TOOLS AND TECHNIQUES
FOR STRUCTURED
SYSTEMS
ANALYSIS AND DESIGN

TOOLS AND TECHNIQUES FOR STRUCTURED SYSTEMS ANALYSIS AND DESIGN

WILLIAM S. DAVIS
MIAMI UNIVERSITY, OXFORD, OHIO

ADDISON-WESLEY PUBLISHING COMPANY

Reading, Massachusetts • Menlo Park, California
London • Amsterdam • Don Mills, Ontario • Sydney

Copyright © 1983 by Addison-Wesley Publishing Company, Inc.

ISBN 0-201-10274-9
ABCDEFGHIJ-AL-89876543

Preface

This book is a collection of seventeen brief tutorials on the tools and techniques of structured systems analysis and design. It is written as a desk reference. Each tutorial describes one tool or technique, shows how it is used, and lists references for those who need more detail. Where appropriate, the rules for using a technique are summarized on a single page for easy access. Each tutorial begins with a topic outline (with page references), and a detailed index can be found in the back of the book. Additionally, other texts referenced in the tutorials are listed on the pages immediately preceeding the index.

Tools and Techniques for Structured Systems Analysis and Design is written for those who already know something about analysis and design, but who cannot afford the time or expense of a professional seminar or a library of current literature. Most of the material is extracted from another text by the author, *Systems Analysis and Design: a Structured Approach* (Addison-Wesley, 1983). This latter book uses case studies to present a structured methodology and current tools and techniques *in the context* of the traditional system life cycle, and is recommended for beginners or for those who want to gain a broad understanding of this most exciting field.

Oxford, Ohio   W.S.D.
February, 1983

Contents

Module A

Inspections and Walkthroughs

OUTLINE

INSPECTIONS AND WALKTHROUGHS

If the systems analysis and design process is to be controlled, we must have a defined event or milestone that occurs at the end of each step in the process. Management review is certainly required, but tends to focus on such factors as cost, return on investment, and schedule, and often lacks technical depth. An *inspection* is a formal review of the exit criteria conducted by technical personnel. The intent of the inspection is to determine the technical accuracy of the exit documentation. When a project passes an inspection, it is assumed that the work up to this point is both technically acceptable and consistent with the objectives of the system. Often, an inspection is used as a prerequisite to a management review.

A *walkthrough* can be viewed as an informal inspection. Before presenting documentation to an inspection team or to management, the analyst is strongly advised to preview the material to several colleagues; such "dry runs" help to identify rough spots, and can save the analyst considerable embarrassment. Although quite valuable at any stage in the systems analysis and design process, walkthroughs are particularly important during the implementation stage as means of checking the accuracy of the code.

THE INSPECTION TEAM

An inspection team normally consists of four individuals: the moderator, the author, and two inspectors. The key member is the *moderator*. Ideally, this individual should be respected technically, and should be unbiased, with no direct involvement in the project. The moderator runs the inspection, scheduling all meetings, distributing all necessary documentation, conducting all sessions, and making certain that the inspection is both thorough and fair. This is a very difficult job, with a significant amount of responsibility.

The *author* is usually the person who wrote the documentation or the code being inspected; if an analysis or programming team is involved, the project leader normally performs this role. The author is expected to answer technical questions, but should refrain from defending the work. It is very difficult for anyone to evaluate his or her own efforts; thus the outside perspectives of the moderator and the inspectors are crucial to the inspection process.

The *inspectors* should be technical professionals who, while not directly involved in preparing the documentation, have a stake in the outcome. The individual who was responsible for the prior step would be a good choice; a member of the group that will subsequently use the output of this step would be another. Normally, two inspectors are assigned; under unusual circumstances, the team can be larger or smaller.

THE INSPECTION PROCESS

The inspection process consists of six steps:

1. planning,

2. overview,

3. preparation,

4. the inspection session,

5. rework,

6. follow-up.

Planning

As soon as the documentation for a given step is completed, the author contacts the moderator and asks that the inspection process begin. The first task is to select an inspection team. In many organizations, the moderator selects the team; in others, management assumes this responsibility. Once the team has been named, the moderator must distribute all materials and schedule the inspection meeting or meetings.

The steps in any well-run project will, of course, be carefully scheduled in advance. The inspection is a key step in this process; if the inspection is late, the project will almost certainly fall behind schedule. Ideally, the inspection should not begin until the author has completed all the documentation; realistically, management will pressure both the author and the moderator to begin on time.

Overview

The overview step is the only optional step in the inspection process. If a project is particularly extensive or involves a number of concepts or techniques that are not apparent to the inspectors, it may be valuable for the author to present a brief technical overview of the project and the documentation. The moderator must control the overview. It should not be allowed to degenerate into a question and answer session, a sales pitch, or a preliminary inspection. The objective is to save the moderator and the inspectors some time. The danger is that the author may bias the other members, making it easy for them to overlook errors. The author's presentation should stick to the facts, stressing what was done and how—not why it was done that way. Later, after the other members of the team have had an opportunity to review and understand the documentation, the reasons behind the technical decisions should be considered.

Preparation

The preparation step calls for individual work on the part of each of the participants. The moderator and the inspectors should read the documentation and note any questions or potential problems. Should the author be asked to answer questions about the project during preparation? Although asking for clarification can save some time, there is a danger that the author may explain away a possible error, and thus bias the inspection process. In some organizations, contact between the inspectors and the author during the preparation step is officially prohibited, but such rules are very difficult to enforce. At the very least the participants should be aware of the potential for bias, and should avoid nonessential contact.

The Inspection Session

The inspection session is conducted by the moderator. One of the inspectors (not the author) is asked to be the reader; this individual reads aloud or paraphrases the documentation. Since paraphrasing involves at least an element of interpretation, it is better than simply reading the material word for word; if the reader paraphrases incorrectly, the documentation is probably unclear, and unclear documentation often accompanies a technical error. During the inspection session, the author's primary responsibility is to answer technical questions.

The objective of the inspection session is to find errors. Note that the inspectors are not to correct these errors; their responsibility is to find them. All participants, including the moderator, the author, and the reader, should inspect the documentation; anyone, including the author, is allowed to identify an error. The moderator maintains an error log (Fig. A.1), noting each error and estimating its severity: trivial, moderate, significant, severe, or fatal. The inspection session should be limited to perhaps 90 minutes, and all participants should be aware of this time limit. If excessive errors are encountered, the moderator has the authority to terminate and reschedule the inspection session; inspecting incomplete or sloppy documentation is a waste of time. Finally, the moderator has the right to schedule a reinspection after rework has been completed.

The moderator must control the inspection process. One danger is that the author will become a proponent or defender of the work, and attempt to discredit any suggestion that an error might be present. At the other extreme, one or more inspectors might become excessively negative, and conduct a "witch hunt" rather than an inspection. It is always possible that one individual may try to dominate the inspection by force of personality. The moderator's job is to see that the inspection is conducted fairly and impartially, and that everyone has an opportunity to participate.

A common point of disagreement involves assigning a measure of severity to each error. The author may see an error as trivial, while an inspector may consider it severe; the result could well be a protracted argument. After a reasonable discussion, the moderator must break in, arbitrarily assign a severity level to the error, and move on. The estimate of severity is, after all, merely a label that is attached to the error. The important thing is that the error be detected; its classification is secondary.

Rework

Following the inspection, the moderator and the author meet to discuss the results; the focus of this meeting is the error list compiled during the inspection session. Each error should be discussed, and the rework time estimated. The responsibility for actually doing the rework belongs to the author. As each error is corrected, the author should note the actual rework time. A key management concern is that rework time be estimated accurately. An inspection data base containing a history of estimated and actual rework tmes can be used to help improve the estimation process.

Follow-up

When the rework is completed, the author and the moderator meet once again to review the results. If the moderator is satisfied with the rework, the inspection process

Fig. A.1: *A typical error log.*

INSPECTION ERROR LOG

PROJECT:_____

MODULE OR COMPONENT: _____
_____
_____

INSPECTION LEVEL: _____

SESSION DATE: _____
TARGET DATE: _____
MODERATOR: _____
AUTHOR: _____
INSPECTOR: _____
_____
_____

	ERROR DESCRIPTION	SEVERITY	EST. TIME	ACT. TIME	DATE COMP.	CHECK
1						
2						
3						
4						
5						
6						
7						
8						
9						
10						
		TOTALS				

INSPECTION TIME

MODERATOR
AUTHOR
INSPECTOR
INSPECTOR
INSPECTOR

TOTAL _____

We have inspected the unit of work described above and have found it technically acceptable.

MODERATOR_____

AUTHOR _____

DATE INSPECTION COMPLETED: _____

INSPECTORS

_____
_____
_____

ends. If not, the moderator may request additional rework and another follow-up session, or perhaps schedule a reinspection. If this is necessary, the inspection team is reconvened, and the inspection session, rework, and follow-up are repeated.

THE INSPECTION AND THE MANAGEMENT REVIEW

Following the successful completion of an inspection, the moderator must "sign-off." Sometimes, a simple memo will suffice. In other organizations, a standard form is completed and signed. Often, the moderator, the author, and the inspectors sign the error list (complete with rework notations) at the end of the process. This formal documentation notifies management that the project has been technically reviewed and found acceptable. In the subsequent management review, technical aspects of the system can be assumed valid, and management can concentrate on costs, benefits, and schedule.

INSPECTION POINTS

In the structured methodology outlined in Module Q, we recommend that formal inspections be conducted at the end of the analysis, system design, detailed design, and implementation steps (Fig. A.2). Problem definition and the feasibility study do not require a formal inspection, as they tend to be very limited in a technical sense; the systems analyst may, however, choose to conduct a walkthrough of the feasibility study before presenting it to management and the user. The implementation step ends with a formal system test, and many organizations consider this test a sufficient check of the technical accuracy of the code. Given this viewpoint, a walkthrough might be enough during implementation.

An inspection marks the end of one phase of the system life cycle. It is usually followed by a management review. The inspection and the review represent the essential defined events or milestones that mark the transition from one stage to another.

The first formal inspection follows completion of the analysis stage (Fig. A.2). The key question to be answered in this first inspection is: Does the analyst really understand the problem? Key documentation includes a data flow diagram, an elementary data dictionary, and brief descriptions of the important algorithms. This documentation should be aimed at the user, and not at the programmer. At this stage, it is important that user representatives be on the inspection team.

The end of the system design phase marks the second inspection point (Fig. A.2). The intent of system design is to set the technical direction for the system; thus both users and programmers should be on the inspection team. In addition to the documentation from the analysis stage, the analyst should identify at least three alternative solutions, and provide system flow diagrams and cost estimates for each; often the analyst will recommend one of these options. The inspection team should review the alternatives as presented, and should make certain that the analyst has not simply bypassed this step by presenting only one serious alternative. Comments on the recommended alternative are certainly in order. The final decision, however, will be made by management.

Fig. A.2: *A summary of key inspection points.*

Analysis: What must be done to solve the problem?

Inspection criteria:	Inspectors:
data flow diagram	users
data dictionary	
algorithms	

Key inspection concerns:
1. Does the analyst *really* understand the problem?
2. Has the analyst defined what must be done to solve the problem?

Objective: To ensure that the analyst is on the right track.

System Design: How, in general, should the problem be solved?

Inspection criteria:	Inspectors:
alternative solutions	users
system flow diagrams	programmers
cost estimates	technical personnel
recommendations	author - analysis

Key inspection concerns:
1. Are the alternative solutions technically realistic?
2. Do the alternatives represent a reasonable choice?
3. Will the alternatives solve the user's problem?

Objective: To set a reasonable technical direction for the system.

Detailed Design: How, specifically, should the system be implemented?

Inspection criteria:	Inspectors:
Hierarchy charts	programmers
IPO charts	author - system design
complete data dictionary	perhaps a user
file specifications	
pseudo code algorithms	
cost estimates	
implementation schedule	
hardware specifications	
rough test plan	

Key inspection concerns:
1. Can the code be written from these specifications?
2. Are the cost estimates and schedule reasonable?
3. Are implementation specifications consistent with the system objectives?

Objective: To ensure that the system will solve the user's problem.

Implementation: Write the code and install the system.

Inspection criteria:	Inspectors:
source listing	programmers
procedures	author - detailed design
	users of procedures
	system users

Key inspection concerns:
1. Does the code meet the specifications?
2. Are the procedures reasonable?

Objective: To ensure that the system as implemented matches the system as planned.

The third inspection follows detailed design (Fig. A.2). The key question at this stage is: Can programming write code based on these specifications? The analyst is expected to provide literally everything the programmers need to write the code—as a minimum, hierarchy charts, input/process/output charts, a complete data dictionary, file specifications, pseudo code versions of the algorithms, cost estimates, and implementation schedules. The inspection team should contain at least one programmer, and probably more. If someone other than the author prepared the system design specifications, that individual should be on the team as well. Following this step, management will be asked to commit sufficient funds to implement the system; thus an in-depth management review can be expected. Note: although our emphasis has been on software development, other exit criteria for the detailed design stage, hardware specifications for example, might be subjected to an inspection as well; it is even possible that different teams of experts might inspect different elements of the documentation.

Several inspections might occur during implementation (Fig. A.2 again). Many organizations use code inspections, with a reader paraphrasing a source listing, while the inspectors look for logical errors. Code walkthroughs might be used in addition to (or in place of) an inspection. A code walkthrough is less formal than an inspection, with teams consisting exclusively of other programmers, and no standard error reporting procedures. Because a system test is normally scheduled at the end of the implementation step, a formal inspection may not be needed.

During implementation, the analyst normally prepares operating procedures, security procedures, auditing procedures, and similar documents. It is important that these be checked. Often, a formal inspection involving the affected people is scheduled for each set of procedures; for example, computer operators may be asked to inspect the operating procedures.

SOME POLITICAL CONSIDERATIONS

Excessive management involvement can destroy the inspection process. A manager's comments tend to take on added significance simply because they come from a manager. If this happens, what should be a technical review process can easily be dominated by non-technical management issues. Given a reasonable level of independence, the inspection process will generate a solid technical review of the project. The fact that the project passed an inspection can then be accepted as proof of its technical soundness, allowing management to concentrate on such issues as cost, benefit, personnel, equipment commitments, and the schedule.

The error reports generated during the actual inspection session represent another point of concern. People naturally fear that an error report will in some way be used against them—that error rates will eventually creep into personnel evaluations. This puts unnecessary pressure on the inspection team. Management must avoid misusing these data.

Another danger is that an analyst or programmer, fearing criticism or the misuse of an error report, wlll simply postpone the inspection until everything is perfect. A project schedule is essential, and the moderator must have the authority to insist that the schedule be followed (within reason), or that the schedule be officially changed. A change in the schedule is, of course, a legitimate reason for management to become involved.

The inspection process puts a great deal of pressure on the moderator. Without management's authority, this individual must perform several management-like functions, including scheduling meetings, conducting meetings and limiting their scope, and, perhaps most significantly, ordering and evaluating rework. The moderator is in a particularly uncomfortable position when a reinspection is required, because the need for reinspection implies that the author did not do a very good job the first time through. Some personal friction is inevitable. In many organizations, a reinspection is made a standard part of the inspection process, and, if the first inspection goes well, the moderator is given the authority to cancel it. As a result, the moderator can make a positive decision rather than a negative one. In effect, the moderator is asked to say "good job" or "no comment" rather than "bad job" or "no comment", a much more confortable choice.

REFERENCES

1. Freedman and Weinberg (1982), *Handbook of Walkthroughs, Inspections, and Technical Reviews.* Boston: Little, Brown and Company, Inc.

2. IBM Corporation (1977), *Inspections in Application Development — Introduction and Implemention Guidelines.* White Plains, New York: IBM Corporation. (IBM publication number GC20-2000.)

Module B

Interviewing

INTERVIEWING

An effective systems analyst must be able to conduct interviews. An interview can be an extremely valuable source of information, particularly during the early feasibility study and analysis stages of the system life cycle. This module is written to give you some general hints on how to conduct an interview.

From the analyst's perspective, the basic reason for conducting an interview is to collect information. As the system life cycle begins, the analyst usually has numerous bits and pieces of information to work with: existing documentation, procedures, and so on. A good analyst can often form a surprisingly complete picture of the existing or proposed system from these sources, but invariably questions and ambiguities will arise, and key pieces will be missing. Only people directly involved in the system can answer these questions, clear up the ambiguities, or supply the missing pieces. Thus, the systems analyst must conduct interviews.

PREPARING FOR THE INTERVIEW

Effective interviewing is the result of careful preparation. Don't "wing it." Know why you want the interview and what you hope to accomplish before you schedule an interview.

Begin by defining the purpose of the interview. Go through the formal documentation, and develop a picture of the existing or proposed system. Identify questions, missing pieces, and ambiguities. These unknown factors or components represent an initial outline of the interview objectives. Note that you may have to interview several people to meet these initial objectives.

Next, *select the person or group to be interviewed.* Obviously, you want to find the individual who can best answer the questions. How do you find this person? Several clues might be used, including the formal organization chart, a work flow analysis, or a report distribution list. Often, the best thing to do is to begin with the organization chart and interview the manager who seems most likely to be responsible for a given objective. Although the manager may not be able to answer specific questions with the required level of detail, he or she should be able to tell you who can. If nothing else, starting with the manager makes political sense; people are less hesitant to give you their time if the boss knows about the interview and has approved it.

Before actually conducting the interview, *do your homework.* Know the topic. Read the relevant documentation. If you are about to interview a manager, know that manager's position on the organization chart, and know the basic functions of that manager's department or group. If you are about to interview a clerical employee, be familiar with the relevant documents or procedures that employee uses. An unprepared interviewer is resented; people do not like to have their time wasted.

Prepare specific questions aimed at the individual (or group) you are planning to interview. Refer to the objectives outline and select all questions that this individual might be able to answer. Develop a written list of questions, and consider follow-up questions to use in case the interview begins straying from the key point. Remember, however, that you can't anticipate everything, so don't try. The list of questions is a guide to the interview, and not an absolute.

Schedule the interview. You need the information. You are asking another person to give up some time. You must be willing to arrange your schedule and to travel to the other person's office or workplace. If you expect cooperation, schedule the interview at the subject's convenience.

THE INTERVIEW ITSELF

A well-conducted interview consists of three distinct parts: an opening, a body, and a closing. Let's consider each of these phases one at a time:

The Opening

The key objective of the opening is to establish rapport. Begin by identifying yourself, the topic you plan to discuss, and the purpose of the interview. Be honest. If there is an established project, you might offer to share the statement of scope and objectives prepared during the problem definition step; even if the subject chooses not to read the statement, its very existence gives the interview an added touch of legitimacy. Tell the individual why he or she was chosen for the interview. Where appropriate, identify the managers who have authorized the interview.

In an attempt to establish a relaxed atmosphere, many good interviewers begin with a brief period of smalltalk by discussing the weather, the exploits of a local sports team, or similar trivia. While this technique can be effective, it can also backfire. If you have an established relationship with the person being interviewed, or if the subject is obviously nervous, a brief period of casual conversation might help. Avoid wasting time, however. When in doubt, get to the point.

The Body

If you are conducting the interview, you are responsible for actually getting things started. Have your first question prepared—an open question, for example:

> When I read the documentation for this system, I had some trouble
> with (mention the part or section). Can you explain it to me?

Or, consider asking the subject how his or her job relates to the project, or how a particular procedure or system works. Ask follow-up questions to help focus the interview. Many people tend to concentrate on how things work; ask why they work as they do. Another effective technique is to say something like: "Let's see if I understand what you're saying", and then offer a brief summary. If your understanding is wrong, the other person will probably correct you; if it's accurate, you establish that effective communication is taking place.

You should generally begin with a relatively broad, open question, and gradually, through increasingly specific follow-up questions, focus the interview on particular points of concern. Often, an individual will explain a detail while reacting to an open question. Also, the interviewer might learn something, getting an answer to an important question that had not been anticipated. This type of questioning is called a funnel sequence.

Listen to the answers. Don't concentrate so intently on your next question that you miss the answer to the current one. (This is a common beginner's mistake.) Be flexible. Try to stick to the subject, but allow a certain amount of spontaneous discussion; you might learn something. Your list of prepared questions (or your objective outline) should be used as a guide or a memory jog, and not as an absolute. Delete questions that seem unimportant, or that, based on earlier responses, you know cannot or will not be answered. Bypass questions that have already been answered. Make sure your questions are relevant. Avoid needlessly complex questions; ask one clear question at a time.

Your attitude toward the interview is important in determining its success or failure. An interview is not a contest. Avoid attacks; avoid excessive use of technical jargon; conduct an interview, not a "snowjob." Talk *to* people, not up to them, down to them, or at them. An interview is not a trial. Do ask probing questions, but don't cross-examine. Remember that the interviewee is the expert, and that you are the one looking for answers. Finally, whatever you do, avoid attacking the other person's credibility. Don't say, "So and so told me something different", or, "You don't know what you're talking about." You will sit through an occasional useless interview. An early closing might be in order, but always act professionally in spite of your disappointment.

Should you take notes during the interview? Unless you have an excellent memory, it is always a good idea to jot down key points, but don't overdo it. Be unobtrusive and selective; it is not necessary to record every word. One suggestion is to leave space for notes on your objective outline or interview outline; if nothing else, a prepared note-taking structure can eliminate the need to write the question during the interview.

Don't be a compulsive note taker. Don't concentrate so much on recording every word, that you miss the meaning. You must listen to the answers. You must be prepared to ask follow-up or probing questions, and you can't do that if your concentration is focused on a piece of note paper. Be honest with yourself. If you feel compelled to take extensive notes, consider taping the interview. A caution: if you plan to use a tape recorder, get the permission of the subject. Also, check out your equipment before the interview, and take along an extra tape or two, just in case.

The Closing

As the interview draws to an end, it is important to maintain a sense of rapport. Pay attention to the time. If the interview runs longer than anticipated, ask permission to continue, and offer to reschedule. When you have all the information you need, thank the subject for cooperating, and offer to make your written summary available for review. If you anticipate the need for a follow-up or subsequent interview with the same person, say so. Some interviewers like to "wind down" with a brief period of casual conversation. If you feel comfortable with this approach, use it; casual conversation is not, however, required—don't force it.

14

FOLLOW-UP

As soon as possible after the interview has ended, transcribe your notes. Ideally, the notes should concentrate on key ideas; use your memory to fill in the details. If you have recorded the interview, listen to the tape and compile a set of selective notes. In either case, have your summary typed, and be sure to identify the person, the date, the place, and the topic of the interview. Share your summary with the interviewee; it's good public relations, and provides an excellent opportunity for correcting misunderstandings.

One or more follow-up interviews may be necessary. If the follow-up involves a single question or two, consider using the telephone. If you anticipate an interview of more than a few minutes, say so, and offer to schedule an appointment.

REFERENCES

1. Stewart, Charles J. and Cash (1978). *Interviewing Principles and Practices, second edition*. Dubuque, Iowa: W.C. Brown.

The Feasibility Study

WHAT IS A FEASIBILITY STUDY?

A feasibility study is a compressed, capsule version of the entire systems analysis and design process. The study begins by clarifying the problem definition. The initial statement of scope and objectives is confirmed or corrected, and any constraints imposed on the system are identified.

Once an acceptable problem definition has been generated, the analyst develops a logical model of the system. A search for alternative solutions then begins, using this model as a reference. Next, the alternatives are carefully analyzed for feasibility. At least three different types of feasibility are considered:

1. *Technical:* Can the system be implemented using current technology?

2. *Economic:* Do benefits outweigh costs?

3. *Operational or organizational:* Can the system be implemented in this organization?

For each feasible solution, the analyst prepares a rough implementation schedule.

The results of the feasibility study are presented to both management and the user. A written report is almost always required, and oral presentations are common. "Drop the project" is one possible recommendation. Assuming that the analyst has found a feasible solution, the feasibility study should provide a broad sense of technical direction for the project; *i.e.*, a plan to proceed.

How much time should be spent on the feasibility study? The answer depends on the project's scope. For a relatively minor change in the format of an existing report, a brief telephone conversation might be adequate. On an estimated quarter million dollar project to develop a new accounting system, a feasibility study of a few weeks would probably be reasonable. For the software company developing a new, multi-million dollar package, it might make sense to spend six months or a year designing and testing a prototype system. The cost of the feasibility study should be approximately 5 to 10 percent of the estimated total project cost.

Over the next several pages, we will outline the steps involved in a typical feasibility study. Use the outline, as a general guideline, but remember that no two systems are exactly the same. The steps describe a feasibility study of several days' duration.

THE STEPS IN A TYPICAL FEASIBILITY STUDY

1. Define the scope and objectives of the system. During problem definition, a statement of scope and objectives was prepared. The analyst should confirm the problem definition, the anticipated scope of the project, and the system objectives. Any constraints should be clearly identified. Interviews with key personnel and a review of written material will certainly be required. Essentially, the analyst is attempting to answer a very simple question: Am I working on the right problem?

2. Study the existing system (if there is one). The existing system is an important source of information. Obviously, if a system is being used, it must be performing some useful work, and its basic functions must be incorporated into the new system. On the other hand, if the existing system were doing a perfect job, there would be no need for a new system; thus, any problems identified in the old system must be corrected. Finally, the cost of operating the existing system represents an economic target; if the new system does not provide additional benefits and/or reduce costs, the old system should be retained.

Carefully analyze written procedures and documentation. Learn the informal system, too. Track the work flow; a good place to start is with the distribution list for any reports generated by the system. Learn what the system does, and why it does it that way. Get cost data; know how much it costs to operate the present system. You will find it necessary to interview people (see Module B). Remember that the relationship between a systems analyst and a user resembles that of a doctor and a patient. The user will often describe symptoms rather than real problems, and the analyst must interpret the information.

A common error is spending too much time analyzing the existing system. The objective is not to document what is done, but to *understand* what is done. The analyst should not be concerned with *how* the existing system works, but should concentrate on *what* it does. Construct a data flow diagram (Module D) and a data dictionary (Module E) for the old system; a high-level system flow diagram (Module F) is another possibility. Do not, however, spend a great deal of time on the implementation details; for example, avoid drawing program logic flowcharts from the code unless you are trying to define a particularly crucial algorithm.

The analyst should get one final piece of information from the present system. Few systems exist in a vacuum; most interface with several others. Define these interfaces; they represent very important constraints on the design of a new system.

3. Develop a high-level logical model of the proposed system. At this point, the analyst should have a good sense of the functions and constraints of the new system. A logical model of the new system can be constructed using a data flow diagram and perhaps a data dictionary. Later, this logical model can be used in designing the new system (Fig. C.1).

4. Redefine the problem in the light of new knowledge. By developing a logical model of the proposed system, the analyst is essentially saying: "Here is what I think the system must do." Does the user agree? It's easy to find out. Ask. At this stage, the analyst should review the problem definition, scope, and objectives with key personnel, using the logical data flow diagram and the data dictionary as a basis for the discussion. If the analyst has misunderstood, or the user has overlooked something, now is the time to find out. Think of the first four steps of the feasibility study as a loop. The analyst defines the problem, analyzes it, develops a tentative solution, redefines the problem, reanalyzes it, revises the solution, and continues this cyclic process until the logical model meets the system objectives.

5. Develop and evaluate alternative solutions. Given a logical model of the proposed system, the analyst can begin to generate high-level, alternative physical solutions. How does an analyst generate these alternatives? Perhaps the easiest approach is to start

Fig. C.1: *Good design begins with the existing physical system, develops a logical model of that system, uses the model to construct a logical model of the proposed system, and then bases the new physical system on that logical model.*

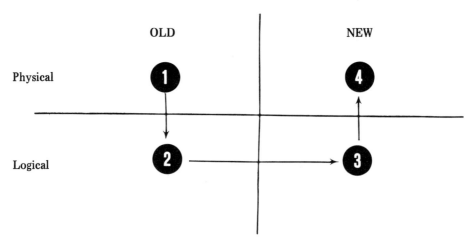

with technical feasibility as a driving mechanism, and to think of a variety of ways in which the problem could be solved. For example, Module D describes the process of identifying automation boundaries on a data flow diagram. Each of these automation boundaries represents one possible physical solution; the analyst might define several sets of automation boundaries, and then determine how the system might be implemented with each set.

Another option is to use a technique known as *brainstorming*. Given the logical model of the system and an hour or two of uninterrupted time, the analyst and a few technical colleagues meet to dream up possible solutions. The rules are simple. Everyone is expected to contribute possible solutions to the problem. No one is allowed to criticize, and no attempt is made to evaluate the suggestions. The point is simply to compile a list of ideas. A brainstorming session might end at a predetermined time, or when a predetermined number of alternatives has been generated. Following the session, the analyst is expected to evaluate the suggestions and select a few that seem reasonable.

Many analysts prefer to use a checklist. For example, several different types of systems might be developed on each of several different types of computers; a few representative examples are summarized in Fig. C.2. At each block in the matrix is a particular type of system—a batch system on a microcomputer, a batch system on a mainframe, an interactive system on a minicomputer, and so on. Using the matrix as a guide, the analyst can attempt to envision a system for each block. Two additional alternatives should always be considered—the existing system and a manual system.

Once a set of technical alternatives has been generated, the initial weeding can be done on the basis of technical feasibility. If, for example, a system requires 3 to 4 second response time, any batch-oriented alternative can be ignored. If the programmers are not trained in interactive programming, the interactive systems might be ruled out. At the end of this process, the analyst should have a set of technically feasible alternatives.

Fig. C.2: *A checklist of system types.*

SOURCE	TYPE	COMPUTER				
		MICRO-COMPUTER	MINI-COMPUTER	MAIN-FRAME	SERVICE BUREAU	TIME-SHARING SERVICE
INTERNAL	BATCH					
	INTERACTIVE					
	REAL-TIME					
EXTERNAL	BATCH					
	INTERACTIVE					
	REAL-TIME					
TURNKEY	BATCH					
	INTERACTIVE					
	REAL-TIME					

EXISTING SYSTEM_____

MANUAL SYSTEM_____

Operational or organizational feasibility might be considered next. For example, the user could be opposed on general principles to an outside service bureau or time-shared service. Another organization might have a bias against a particular vendor's hardware, or for a particular type of system. Company policy or a union agreement might dictate either for or against a particular option. Basically, the analyst should check each remaining alternative against the way the organization does business, and eliminate any that might be operationally unacceptable.

Consider economic feasibility next. Estimate both the development and operating cost of each remaining alternative. Estimate the cost savings and/or revenue increase relative to the existing system (if there is one). Perform a cost/benefit analysis for each alternative (see Module G). Only those alternatives that promise a positive return on investment should be considered further.

Finally, for each alternative that passes the technical, operational, and economic feasibility tests, develop an implementation schedule. This schedule does not have to be detailed; tie it to the system life cycle, and estimate the date of completion for each phase.

6. *Decide on a recommended course of action.* The key decision arising from the feasibility study is whether to continue or to drop the project. Indicate this essential "go/no go" recommendation clearly. Assuming that the recommendation is to continue with the project, the analyst should select the best alternative, and justify that choice. It is important to remember that management must constantly consider alternative sources for investment, and that developing a new system is a form of investment. If the best alternative for the proposed system offers a projected return on investment of 15 percent, and the prime interest rate is 16 percent, management may

Fig. C.3: *An outline of a typical feasibility study.*

A. **TITLE PAGE.** *Project name, report title, author(s), date.*

B. **CONTENTS.** *A list of report sections with page numbers.*

C. **PROBLEM DEFINITION.** *A clear, concise, one-page description of the problem.*

D. **EXECUTIVE SUMMARY.** *A clear, concise, one-page summary of the feasibility study, the results, and the recommendations. Include necessary authorizations, key sources of information, alternatives considered, and alternatives rejected. Highlight the costs, benefits, constraints, and time schedule associated with the recommended alternative.*

E. **METHOD OF STUDY.** *A reasonably detailed description of the approach and procedures used in conducting the feasibility study. Mention your sources and references, and identify key people. Briefly describe the existing system (if appropriate). Much of the detail belongs in the appendix (see item J): include only those facts directly relevant to the study or to your conclusions.*

F. **ANALYSIS.** *A high-level analysis of the proposed logical system. Include a statement of the system objectives, constraints, and scope; it should be more detailed than the one developed during problem definition. Include a logical data flow diagram and perhaps an elementary data dictionary for the proposed system. Identify key interrelationships with other systems.*

G. **ALTERNATIVES CONSIDERED.** *For each alternative seriously considered, include a statement of its technical feasibility, economic feasibility, operational feasibility, a rough implementation schedule, and a high-level system flow diagram or other system description. Be thorough, but don't overdo it—much of the detail belongs in the appendix.*

H. **RECOMMENDATIONS.** *Clearly state the recommended course of action. Provide material to support and justify your recommendation; in particular, provide a cost/benefit analysis.*

I. **DEVELOPMENT PLAN.** *Include a projected schedule and projected costs for each step in the system life cycle, assuming that the recommended course of action is followed. Provide detailed time and cost estimates for the next step in the process—analysis.*

J. **APPENDIX.** *Charts, graphs, statistics, interview lists, selected interview summaries, diagrams, memos, notes, references, key contacts, acknowledgements, and so on; in short, the details that support the study. Consider making the appendix available on a demand or need basis.*

well choose to put its money into Treasury bills rather than into this project. Occasionally, a project is justified on non-economic grounds; for example, if new laws or a new union contract make the payroll system obsolete, a new system must be developed. Generally, however, investment decisions are based on the expected returns, so always include a cost/benefit analysis (Module G).

7. *Rough out a development plan.* Assuming that management will accept the recommended course of action, develop an implementation schedule. Estimate personnel requirements, and indicate when analysts, programmers, technical writers, and others will be needed. Estimate the cost of each stage in the system life cycle. Finally, provide a clear, detailed schedule and a set of cost estimates for the next stage—analysis.

8. *Write the feasibility study.* An outline of a typical feasibility study is illustrated in Fig. C.3. Remember that all feasibility studies are different; this outline is intended to be used as a guideline only.

9. *Present the results to management and the user.* The decision to commit funds to the project must be made by management, and not by the analyst.

REFERENCES

The sources listed below take a somewhat different view of feasibility studies, but might prove interesting:

1. Clifton, David S. and Fyffe (1977). *Project Feasibility Analysis: A Guide to Profitable New Ventures.* New York: John Wiley and Sons, Inc.

2. Fitzgerald, J., Fitzgerald, and Stallings (1981). *Fundamentals of Systems Analysis, second edition.* New York: John Wiley and Sons, Inc.

Data Flow Diagrams

DATA FLOW DIAGRAMS

During the early stages of the systems analysis and design process, the analyst collects a great deal of relatively unstructured data from such sources as interviews, written memos, documentation manuals, notes, and even casual conversation. It is important that all this data be summarized. Ideally, this summary should serve a variety of functions. It should simplify communication with the user, and should be useful in supporting the future development of the system. Also, the summary should not force the analyst into premature physical design decisions. The analyst needs something analogous to the architect's preliminary sketches.

A data flow diagram is a logical model of a system. The model does not depend on hardware, software, data structure, or file organization: there are no physical implications in a data flow diagram. Because the diagram is a graphic picture of the logical system, it tends to be easy for even nontechnical users to understand, and thus serves as an excellent communication tool. Finally, a data flow diagram is a good starting point for system design.

CONSTRUCTING A DATA FLOW DIAGRAM

A data flow diagram uses four basic symbols to form a picture of a logical system (Fig. D.1). A square defines a *source* or *destination* of data. A rectangle with rounded corners (some experts use a circle) represents a *process* that transforms data. An open-ended rectangle is a *data store*. An arrow is used to identify a *data flow*.

Note that a process is not necessarily a program. A single process might represent a series of programs, a single program, or a module in a program; it might even represent a manual process, such as keypunching or the visual verification of data. Note also that a data store is not the same as a file. A data store might represent a file, a piece of a file, elements on a data base, or even a portion of a record. A data store might reside on disk, drum, magnetic tape, main memory, microfiche, punched card, or any other medium (including a human brain).

What is the difference between a data store and a data flow? A data flow is data in motion; a data store is data at rest. In other words, they are simply two different states of the same thing. We'll return to this idea later.

Typically, a number of simplifying assumptions are made on a data flow diagram. For example, error processing or handling unusual conditions is ignored, as are housekeeping functions such as opening and closing files. No attention is paid to how the data are processed, or how the data flow from process to process. The point is to describe what happens, without worrying about how it happens.

With traditional logic flowcharts, the direction of flow is from top to bottom and from left to right. A good data flow diagram tends to follow a similar convention, with data moving from its source (at the upper left) to its destination (at the lower right), but the rules are much less rigid. For example, data sometimes flow back to a source. One way to indicate this is to draw a long flowline from one side of the diagram to the other. As an alternative, the symbol for the data source might simply be repeated (Fig. D.2)—in other words, the same symbol representing the same data

Fig. D.1:   *Data flow diagram symbols.*

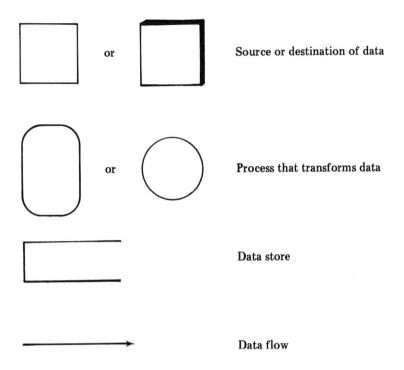

source can appear more than once on a data flow diagram. On a traditional flowchart, repeating a block of logic is considered poor form; on a data flow diagram, if repeating a symbol improves the clarity of the diagram, fine. To avoid possible misunderstanding, a symbol that is used more than once is normally marked with a short diagonal line in one corner; note, for example, the squares labeled *User* in Fig. D.2. Data stores are sometimes repeated, too.

AN EXAMPLE

Perhaps the best way to introduce data flow diagrams is in the context of a simple example. Imagine that the purchasing department needs a daily inventory exception report listing, by part number, all items to be reordered to replenish stock. For each reorder item, purchasing requires: the part number, part description, reorder quantity, current price, primary supplier, and secondary supplier. An item is reordered when the stock on hand drops below a critical level. Inventory transactions (additions and deletions) are reported to the system as they happen through a CRT terminal located in the warehouse. Purchasing wants its list once a day, at the start of business. We'll assume that this simple description of the system requirements has been distilled by the systems analyst from a number of memos, interviews, telephone conversations, and documentation manuals.

Fig. D.2: *A symbol can be repeated on a data flow diagram. When a symbol is used more than once, it is normally marked with a diagonal slash.*

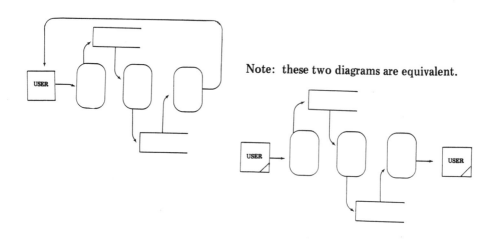

Note: these two diagrams are equivalent.

How does the analyst begin developing a data flow diagram? What are the components of a data flow diagram? There are four: sources or destinations, processes, data stores, and data flows. Thus, the first step is to extract the components from the description. Let's start with data sources and destinations (Fig. D.3). Reread the problem description. Clearly, purchasing needs the report; thus *purchasing* is a data destination. Keep reading. Inventory transactions are reported . . . through a CRT terminal located in the warehouse. That terminal is a source of data; let's identify the source as *warehouse*.

There are no more sources or destinations in the problem description, so we move on to processes. Read the problem description once again. Purchasing needs a report. Clearly, they do not yet have that report, so it must be generated: *generate report* is one process (Fig. D.3).

We must also process inventory transactions. Right now, there might be plenty of stock on hand for part number 123. A few minutes from now, however, a transaction might cause several units of this part to be shipped, and thus removed from inventory; this changes the stock on hand. A process is anything that changes or transforms data. Since the inventory transaction changes the stock on hand, processing that transaction belongs on the data flow diagram. Note that the problem description did not explicitly mention the need to process inventory transactions; the systems analyst must frequently interpret the specifications.

Now, let's consider data stores and data flows. Reread the problem description. The *exception report* is certainly a data flow; Fig. D.3 summarizes the data elements

The elements that make up a data flow diagram can be extracted from descriptive information.

Source/Destination	Process
Purchasing	Generate Report
Warehouse clerk	Process Transaction*

Data Flow	Data Store
Exception report	REORDER
part number	see exception report
part description	
reorder quantity	INVENTORY*
current price	part number*
primary supplier	stock-on-hand
secondary supplier	reorder level
Transaction	
part number*	
transaction type	
transaction quantity*	*by implication

making up the report. *Inventory transactions* come from the warehouse; thus we have another data flow. There is an obvious timing mismatch between processing the inventory transactions and generating the exception report—note that transactions are processed as they occur, and the report is generated only once a day. The data making up an exception report must be held for a time, giving us a data store.

Not all data stores and data flows can be extracted directly from the problem description; some are merely implied. For example, the fact that "an item must be reordered when the stock on hand drops below a critical level" implies that the stock on hand and the critical reorder level must exist somewhere. Since these data elements would seem to exist for a period of time longer than a single transaction, it is reasonable to assume that there must be a data store holding inventory data. In Fig. D.3, data elements that are implied by the system description are identified by an asterisk.

Getting Started

Once the component parts have been isolated, the analyst can begin drawing the data flow diagram. It is best to start at a very high level (Fig. D.4), showing the entire system as a single logical process and clearly identifying the sources and destinations of

Fig. D.4: *A high-level data flow diagram, highlighting data sources and destinations.*

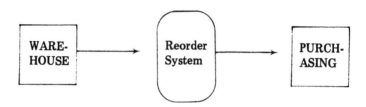

data. Although none are shown here, most systems will interface with other systems, and those other systems should be shown as data sources or destinations.

Even at this very high level, the data flow diagram is most useful as a communication tool. Has the analyst correctly identified all the data sources and destinations? Based only on written and oral documentation, this is not always an easy question to answer; all too often, details can be overlooked. With a high-level data flow diagram, however, the presence or absence of a given data source or destination can be verified (by the user or management) at a glance.

Exploding to a Major Function Level

Fig. D.4 represents perhaps the highest possible view of the system. Except for highlighting data sources and destinations, however, this data flow diagram is not particularly useful. The next step is to "explode" the process into its functional parts. To do this, we must refer back to the list of elements derived from the problem statement (Fig. D.3). Two processes were identified: *generate report* and *process transaction*. These two processes represent the basic functions that must be performed by the system; they will replace *reorder system* in Fig. D.4. Exploding a data flow diagram means replacing a high-level process with its lower-level components (Fig. D.5).

Note that two data stores have been added to the new data flow diagram. *Process transactions* needs inventory data; thus the data store known as *inventory*. Remember the difference in timing between processing the inventory transactions and generating the reorder report? Because of this difference, reorder information must be stored; Thus the *reorder* data store.

Fig. D.5 illustrates several conventions used in drawing a data flow diagram. Processes are numbered for easy reference. Data stores are labeled with "D" followed by a

Fig. D.5: *A functional level data flow diagram.*

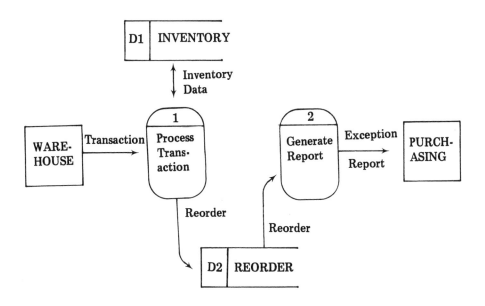

number; again, these labels are for reference only. The names of the data stores, sources, and destinations are written in all capital letters, while the process and data flow names are, except for the first letter, written in lower case. These conventions help to make the data flow diagram easier to follow.

The names of the various data flows are written on the data flow diagram (Fig. D.5). Like the processes, sources, destinations, and data stores, they are derived from the problem description (see Fig. D.3 again). Consider one of those data flows—*reorder*. Is *reorder* a data flow or a data store? At first glance, distinguishing between stores and flows may seem confusing. Don't worry about it. A data flow is data in motion; a data store is data at rest. What elements are found in a data store? Only those elements that entered the data store through a data flow. In other words, a data store and a data flow are just two different versions of the same thing.

Exploding the Major Functions

Once the major functions have been identified and incorporated into the data flow diagram, the analyst can begin to explode each of these functions to a lower level of detail. For example, consider the *process transactions* function of Fig. D.5. Logically, it might be reasonable to break this process into three steps (Fig. D.6): *accept transaction*, *update inventory*, and *process reorder*. Why these three steps? Think about the logical flow of data through the system. First, the transaction must occur and be accepted. Next the transaction can be processed. Finally, once the processing step has determined that a reorder is necessary, the reorder data can be processed. The three steps must occur in the prescribed order. They are relatively independent, linked only

31

Fig. D.6: The data flow diagram with the "process transactions" process exploded to a lower level.

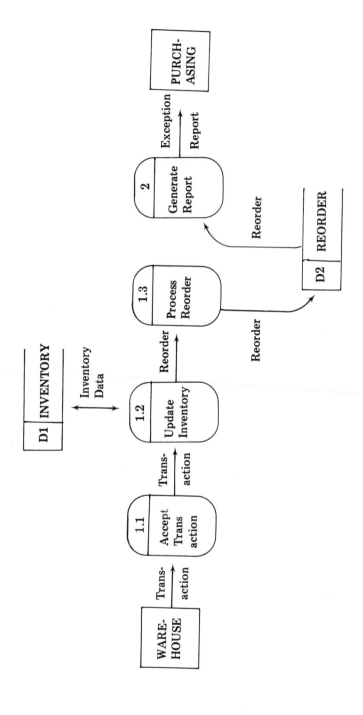

by a data flow. A similar breakdown can be imagined for many functional-level processes.

Note how the processes have been numbered on the exploded data flow diagram. Processes 1.1, 1.2, and 1.3 are component parts of what was process 1. If process 2 were to be exploded, its components would be numbered 2.1, 2.2, and so on.

Should we explode the second process, *generate report*? No. It is relatively easy to visualize what a report generation process will do. Although you might imagine a number of different ways to generate a report using a sort or some other sequencing mechanism, such details involve physical specifications, and are inappropriate on a data flow diagram.

Should we explode any of the processes shown in Fig. D.6 to an even lower level? Probably not. Why? How do you know when you have gone far enough? Consider process 1.1, *accept transaction*. Try to imagine breaking down that process without thinking about how you are going to accept transactions, or where (physically) those transactions are going to come from. When you reach the point where further subdivision forces you to think about how you are going to implement the process, you have gone far enough.

How detailed should a data flow diagram be? The example presented in this module is relatively trivial; what if the data flow diagram contained dozens of processes and data stores? Such a diagram would be very difficult to follow, thus defeating a primary purpose of the data flow diagram—communication. A number of studies suggest that human beings find it difficult to follow a data flow diagram containing more than 7±2 processes. These studies suggest a strategy. Start with a high level diagram. Explode it to a functional level. If exploding all the functions to their next level of detail would cause you to exceed the 9 process limit, don't explode the data flow diagram. Instead, take each function, one at a time, and develop a sub-diagram, showing only the explosion of the single process. Repeat this step for each process. The functional level data flow diagram can then be used to provide a logical overview of the entire system. If a user or a manager wants to know what happens within a given process, the appropriate sub-diagram can be shown.

CHECKING THE DATA FLOW DIAGRAM

Once you have completed a data flow diagram, how can you be sure that it is a reasonable model of the system? The key is to check it with the user, but the analyst can do several things first. For example, remember that the data flows define the minimum contents of the data stores. For any given data store, check the data inflows against the data outflows. The data store should contain all data elements flowing in, and all data elements flowing out. What if it doesn't? What if an element of data that did not flow into a data store flows out? Something is missing. Perhaps the analyst has missed an interface with another system. Perhaps a process is missing. What if a data element flows into a data store, but does not flow out? That data element might be redundant or unnecessary. Perhaps the function that should process the element of data has been overlooked.

Consider, for example, the data store named *inventory*. It provides such data elements as the stock on hand and the reorder level to process 1.2; where did those data elements come from? Obviously, there must be a source for this data, and the source is not shown on Fig. D.6. The explanation may be very simple: inventory master data already exists to support another inventory system. Adding this detail to the data flow diagram may do more harm than good, but the point still remains: there is an inconsistency on the data flow diagram, and that inconsistency must be explained.

The *exception report* provides another example of how checking the data flows can help to improve the system definition. It contains such fields as a part description, a reorder quantity, current price, primary supplier, and secondary supplier. Where do these fields come from? Follow the data flows. Clearly, there is only one possible source: the data store named *inventory*. These data elements should be added to *inventory* and to the data flow named *inventory data*.

Another good idea is to cross-check the different data stores looking for data redundancies; often, two or more data stores can be combined. Although a data flow diagram does not imply physical implementation, some people do tend to view data stores as files. Don't let your data flow diagram even suggest a bad physical implementation.

Be prepared to modify your data flow diagram; in fact, you may need three or four drafts before you even begin to draw the final version. Start with freehand drawings on a note pad, and discuss them with the user. Only when you are confident that the data flow diagram is accurate should you consider using a flowcharting template and ink. People don't like to throw away what they have created. If you draw a data flow diagram using a template and ink, and then discover that something is wrong, there is a danger that you will try to change the system to fit the model. Even experienced analysts do this; it's a natural human reaction. Recognize this temptation, and fight it, even if the error is not your fault.

USING THE DATA FLOW DIAGRAM

The data flow diagram serves a variety of purposes. First, it helps the analyst to organize the information about a system. The very act of creating a data flow diagram forces the analyst to summarize information, extract key details, and consider the relationships among those details. Missing elements that might be overlooked in a massive narrative are often highlighted in the graphic structure of the diagram. Additionally, the contents of the data flows and the data stores represent a base for developing a data dictionary (see Module E).

A data flow diagram is an excellent communication tool. The limited number of symbols and the lack of physical implementation details makes a data flow diagram accessible to most users. In the early planning stages, a rough sketch of a data flow can help to summarize the results of an interview or the contents of formal documentation. Later, a completed data flow diagram can be used to explain the analyst's understanding of a system. An excellent formal presentation technique is to begin with a data flow diagram that has all the symbols in place, and then write the appropriate labels on the sources, destinations, processes, data flows, and data stores as you follow the flow through the system.

The data flow diagram can also be used as a design aid. Using the timing requirements of the various processes as a guide, it is possible to draw a number of different automation boundaries on a diagram, and each automation boundary might suggest a different physical system. Consider Fig. D.6. Transactions occur continuously; thus process 1.1, *accept transaction*, must be on-line. Purchasing wants its report once a day, and thus process 2 would logically run in batch mode. The other processes, however, are not constrained by the problem description. For example, what if we were to accept transactions on-line and enqueue them, updating inventory, processing reorders, and generating the reorder report in a batch mode (Fig. D.7)? We would, of course, need a new data store for the transactions, but our data flow diagram would certainly support this option.

Change the automation boundaries. Enclose processes 1.1, 1.2, and 1.3 within a common boundary (Fig. D.8). Now our system would accept transactions, update inventory, process reorders, and output a reorder record on-line; process 2 would then prepare a reorder report in batch mode. Can you imagine any other automation boundaries? Would it not be possible to group processes 1.1 and 1.2, and then draw a separate boundary around 1.3 and 2? Imagine designing the on-line inventory update module to flag reorders. Later in batch mode, *process reorder* would search *inventory*

Fig. D.7: *Automation boundaries suggesting a batch inventory update.*

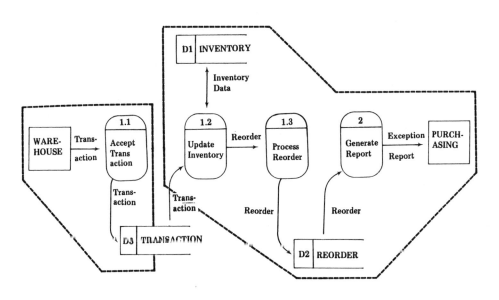

Fig. D.8: *Different automation boundaries suggesting an on-line inventory update.*

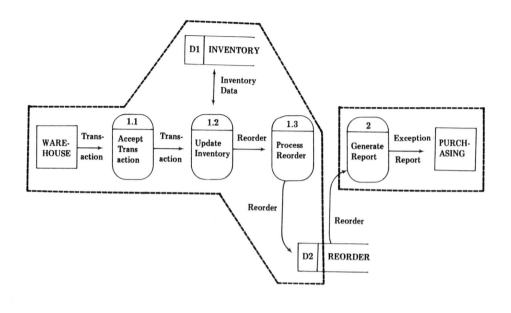

for flagged parts, and send them to *generate report*. Why not enclose all four processes within a single automation boundary and print reorder data in the purchasing department as the reorder condition occurs? Playing with the data flow diagram can allow the analyst to generate a number of reasonable alternative solutions to the problem.

Data flow diagrams can be used even in the detailed design stage. Assume, for example, that an on-line inventory update module will be developed as part of the system. What functions must be performed by this module? Although we are well beyond the logical design stage, we can still use the symbols and rules associated with data flow diagrams to develop a logical model of the program. It is relatively easy to move from a logical model of the data flow through a program to a high-level hierarchy chart of that program (see Module H).

Finally, the data flow diagram can be used to test the early physical design of a system. For example, imagine that a set of hierarchy charts and their associated input/process/output charts has been developed for each of the programs in a system, and that the necessary files have been specified. Each element of the system should have its logical equivalent on the data flow diagram. Do the necessary elements all exist? Are there any extra elements? Next, using the data flow diagram as a base, the analyst can actually trace the flow of data through the physical system. Is anything missing? Have any extra, unnecessary features been added between the analysis and design stages? The data flow diagram does not, of course, anticipate every detail of the physical system, but it is a very good guide to that system.

REFERENCES

1. Gane, Chris and Sarson (1979). *Structured Systems Analysis: Tools and Techniques.* Englewood Cliffs, New Jersey: Prentice-Hall, Inc.

2. Yourdon, Edward and Constantine (1979). *Structured Design.* Englewood Cliffs, New Jersey: Prentice-Hall, Inc.

Data Dictionaries

WHAT IS A DATA DICTIONARY?

A data dictionary is a collection of data about data. The basic idea is to provide information on the definition, structure, and use of each data element an organization uses. A data element is a unit of data that cannot be decomposed. Fig. E.1 summarizes the information that might be stored in a data dictionary.

Fig. E. 1: *A list of information typically recorded for*

each data element on a data dictionary.

General
  Name
  Aliases or synonyms
  Description

Format
  Data type
  Length
  Picture
  Units (lbs/in^2, etc.)

Usage Characteristics
  Range of values
  Frequency of use
  Input/output/local
  Conditional values

Control Information
  Source
  Date of origin
  Users
  Programs in which used
  Change authorizations
  Access authorizations

Group Information
  Parent structure
  Subsidiary structures
  Repetitive structures
  Physical location
    Record
    File
    Data Base

Why use a data dictionary? Perhaps the most obvious reason is documentation; a collection of data about data would be a valuable reference in any organization. Documentation, however, is often promoted for its own sake. What makes a data dictionary so valuable?

Throughout an organization, different people or groups may define a given element of data quite differently. All too often, the analyst and the user will seem to agree on the objectives and scope of a system, only to discover later that they were not really talking about the same thing. Consider, for example, the number of students attending your school. To some, this data element implies a simple head count. To others, it represents the result of a computation: divide total student credit hours by the normal full-time student load to get full-time equivalent students. These numbers can be quite different, particularly at a school with many commuters. Two people can discuss something as "obvious" as the number of students attending a school and have very different ideas in mind. This problem is common. A data dictionary can help to improve analyst/user communication by establishing a set of consistent definitions.

The data dictionary can have more far-reaching implications as well. Consider, for example, a large program involving the efforts of several programmers. If all programmers are required to develop data descriptions from a common data dictionary, a number of potentially serious module interface problems can be avoided. At an even higher level, different systems must often be linked or interfaced. In general, a data dictionary can help to improve communications between broad segments of an organization, simply by providing a set of consistent definitions for the data.

As a new application is being developed, the systems analyst can check the required data elements against the organization's central data dictionary. Some data elements will already exist, and using their established names and formats can save the analyst a great deal of work—why reinvent the wheel? By highlighting already existing elements, a data dictionary can help the analyst to avoid data redundancy, a problem that occurs when a given element of data is physically stored in several different places, under several different formats, and with slightly different levels of control.

Perhaps the most concrete, short run advantage of a data dictionary is derived from the control information that is maintained for each data element (Fig. E.1). Normally, all programs using a given element are cross-referenced in the data dictionary. Thus it becomes very easy to assess the impact of a change in the data. Consider, for example, the proposed nine-digit zip code. With a data dictionary, a complete list of all programs that use the zip code can be quickly compiled, and these programs can all be scheduled for revision. Without a data dictionary, however, there is no way even to identify all programs that use the zip code. Instead, except for a few obvious programs, necessary changes are made haphazardly at best. Often, the fact that a program uses the newly changed data element is not discovered until that program fails.

Finally, a data dictionary is a valuable first step in developing a data base. In fact, many data base management systems include a data dictionary as a standard feature.

DATA DICTIONARY SOFTWARE

A number of data dictionary software packages are commercially available. Some are associated with a specific data base management system. Others are more general; many offer optional links to a variety of data base management systems. Some firms have even written their own customized data dictionary software.

What facilities might you expect to find in a typical data dictionary package? Since creating the data dictionary can be tedious, most contain data entry support. A few are designed to prepare at least part of the entry from programmer source code, a most valuable option when an established computer center decides to install a data dictionary. Another common approach is to display a dummy data dictionary entry on a CRT screen and allow the operation to enter missing elements; other systems use a conversational approach to help the analyst, programmer, or technical writer enter the data about the data.

Many data dictionary systems are designed to generate source code for application programs. The analyst normally checks each data element against the data dictionary. If the element already exists, its name and format will be on the data dictionary, and generating the source code to describe that data element is a relatively simple task. If the data element is new, it can be added to the data base as part of the crosschecking process; once again, generating the source code should be easy. Often, the output from the data dictionary system will be in the form of COBOL DATA DIVISION entries, PL/1 DECLARE statements, or similar data descriptions. The analyst might place this code on a source statement library so that the programmers can simply insert it into their programs.

Earlier, we discussed the possibility of using the control information recorded on a data dictionary to generate a list of all the programs that access a particular data element. Several other data usage reports and cross reference checks might be imagined as well. Many data dictionary software packages include a query feature that allows a user to request specific information about data use. This ability to have the computer investigate how data are used may well be the most valuable feature of a data dictionary.

A SIMULATED DATA DICTIONARY

Data dictionary software is not always available. Another problem with many commercial data dictionaries is that they tend to be linked to a specific data base management system. Thus, we will use a simulated data dictionary to illustrate basic concepts.

Many advantages associated with a data dictionary are derived from the ability to process information about each data element separately. Simply listing all the data elements on a sheet of paper will not do, as it is difficult to deal with the individual elements when they are presented in list form. To maintain a semblance of direct access, information related to each data element will be recorded on a separate 3x5 filing card.

A minimum amount of information will be recorded for each data element (Fig. E.2). The data name will come first. It is a good idea to establish a set of conventions for assigning data names; we'll borrow from the COBOL language, although any other programming language would do as well. Often, a given element of data will be known by more than one name; thus any aliases or synonyms will be recorded. Next comes a brief description or definition of the data element, followed by its type and format. Finally, information related to the physical location of the data element will be recorded. Control information and usage characteristics (if available) will be noted on the back of the card. This control information is more important than its position would seem to indicate, but realistically, we will not be able to perform a large scale cross reference analysis on data recorded on 3x5 cards.

It is easy to overdo the data dictionary. Too many systems analysts, when faced with such a data collection task, tend to lose sight of the real objective. During the early feasibility study and analysis stages, not all the information demanded by a data dictionary will be available. If the analyst "hides behind" the requirement that he or she complete a data dictionary, nothing may really get done. Use the data dictionary as a structure for collecting data about the data. As key bits of information become available, add them to the developing data dictionary. Don't try to predefine everything; you won't be able to do it. In fact, many systems analysts use something like the simulated data dictionary as a note pad to record details as they are uncovered. When

Fig. E.2:   *The minimum information to be collected for each*

data element on the simulated data dictionary.

Name:

Aliases:

Description:

Format:

Location:

---

the time comes to add the information to the computerized data dictionary, these notes will contain most of the necessary information.

AN EXAMPLE

In Module D, a number of data flow diagram concepts were illustrated through a simple example. We might use the same example to illustrate several data dictionary concepts as well. Purchasing needs a daily inventory exception report listing, by part number, all items to be reordered to replenish stock. For each reorder item, purchasing needs: the part number, part description, reorder quantity, most current price, primary supplier, and secondary supplier. An item must be reordered when the stock on hand drops below a critical level. Inventory transactions (additions and deletions) are reported as they happen, through CRT terminals located in the warehouse. Purchasing requires its list once a day, at the start of business.

Let's concentrate on the data elements making up the inventory exception report. We cannot derive all necessary information from the problem definition, but we can at least lay out a skeleton data dictionary (Fig. E.3). The analyst might know a few details from personal experience. Discussions with the user might help to fill in many of the blanks. We might search the existing organizational data dictionary to see if a given element is used in another application; if it is, we can use the established information to describe the element. Missing information serves to alert the analyst that work remains to be done. The data dictionary eventually will be completed, as a direct result of the systems analysis and design process.

Fig. E.3: *A portion of the simulated data dictionary for the inventory example.*

Name: INVENTORY-EXCEPTION-REPORT

Aliases: REORDER-REPORT. PURCHASING-REPORT

Description: Group item representing daily list of parts to be reordered. Sent to purchasing. See back of card for structure.

Format: Group item.

Location: output to printer

Name: PART-NUMBER

Aliases:

Description: Key field that uniquely identifies a specific part in inventory.

Format: Alphanumeric; 8 characters.
PIC X(8).

Location: INVENTORY-EXCEPTION-REPORT
INVENTORY
REORDER

Name: REORDER-QUANTITY

Aliases:

Description: The numer of units of a given part that are to be reordered at a single time.

Format: numeric; 5 digits.
PIC 9(5)

Location: INVENTORY-EXCEPTION-REPORT
INVENTORY
REORDER

44

REFERENCES

1. Atre, S. (1980). *Data Base: Structured Techniques for Design, Performance, and Management.* New York: John Wiley and Sons.

2. Kroenke (1977). *Database Processing.* Chicago: SRA.

3. Lomax, J.D. (1977). *Data Dictionary Systems.* Rochelle Park, New Jersey: NCC Publications. Also distributed by Hayden Book Co.

System Flowcharts

47

SYSTEM FLOWCHARTS

In the structured approach to systems analysis and design, we begin by constructing a logical model, often using data flow diagrams as a tool. During system design, this logical model must be converted to physical form. How do we describe the physical stystem? Remember that we are just beginning to move from the logical to the physical, and are not yet ready to begin specifying details. What we need is an overview.

A system flowchart is a traditional tool for describing a physical system. The basic idea is to provide a symbol to represent, at a black box level, each discrete component in the system—programs, files, forms, procedures, and so on. While a few of the symbols are the same, system flowcharts are quite different from program logic flowcharts (see Module J). A system flowchart is a high-level picture of a physical system.

Fig. F.1:   *Basic flowcharting symbols.*

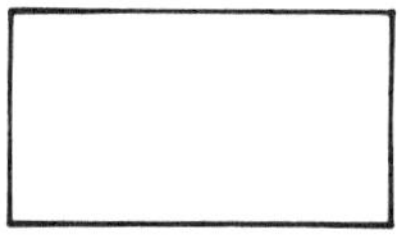 ☐	Process	A process or component that changes the value or location of data. Examples include a program, a processor, and a clerical process.
 ▱	Input/output	A generalized, device independent symbol for input, output, or both.
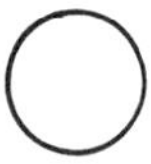 ◯	Connector	Indicates an exit to or entry from another part of the flow-chart, usually on the same page.
 ⬠	Off-page connector	Indicates an exit to or entry from another page of the chart.
→	Flowline	Used to link symbols. The flowlines define both sequence and direction of flow.

FLOWCHARTING SYMBOLS

When a system flowchart is drawn, a separate symbol is used for each discrete component in the system. The basic symbols are shown in Fig. F.1. At first, the analyst may work almost exclusively with the basic symbols. Eventually, however, the general input and output operations must become specific files or data bases stored on specific devices, and the processes must become specific programs or manual procedures. The system flowcharting symbols (Fig. F.2) allow the analyst to represent the actual devices or processes that make up the system.

Fig. F.2: *System flowcharting symbols.*

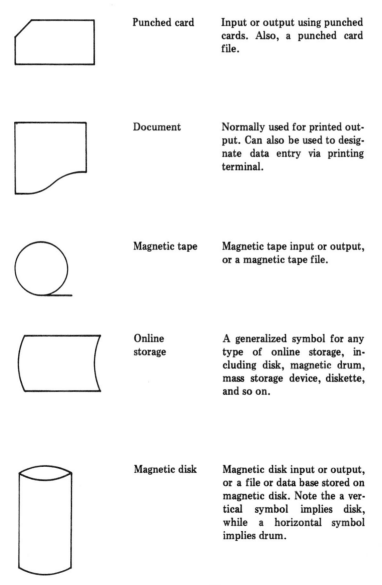

	Punched card	Input or output using punched cards. Also, a punched card file.
	Document	Normally used for printed output. Can also be used to designate data entry via printing terminal.
	Magnetic tape	Magnetic tape input or output, or a magnetic tape file.
	Online storage	A generalized symbol for any type of online storage, including disk, magnetic drum, mass storage device, diskette, and so on.
	Magnetic disk	Magnetic disk input or output, or a file or data base stored on magnetic disk. Note the a vertical symbol implies disk, while a horizontal symbol implies drum.

49

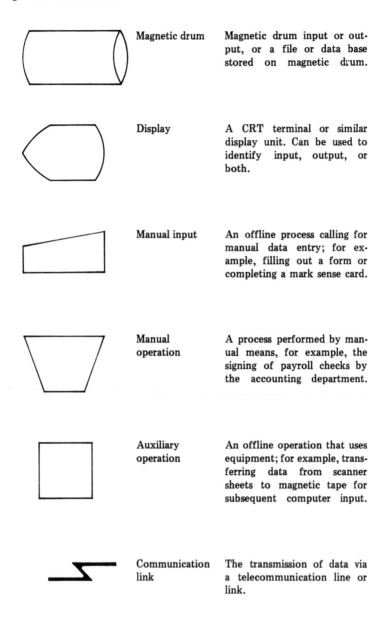

	Magnetic drum	Magnetic drum input or output, or a file or data base stored on magnetic drum.
	Display	A CRT terminal or similar display unit. Can be used to identify input, output, or both.
	Manual input	An offline process calling for manual data entry; for example, filling out a form or completing a mark sense card.
	Manual operation	A process performed by manual means, for example, the signing of payroll checks by the accounting department.
	Auxiliary operation	An offline operation that uses equipment; for example, transferring data from scanner sheets to magnetic tape for subsequent computer input.
	Communication link	The transmission of data via a telecommunication line or link.

AN EXAMPLE

Perhaps the best way to introduce system flowcharts is through a simple example. In Modules D and E, a logical model of a system to solve an inventory problem was developed. One alternative physical solution is illustrated in the system flowchart of Fig. F.3. Read the chart from top to bottom. Transactions enter the system through CRT terminals (the display symbol), and are processed by an inventory program.

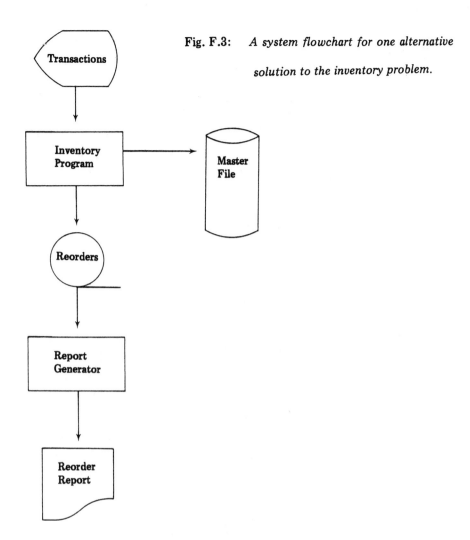

Fig. F.3: *A system flowchart for one alternative solution to the inventory problem.*

The inventory program updates the inventory master file (on disk), and writes necessary reorder information to magnetic tape. Eventually, this tape is read by a report generator program, and the reorder report is printed. Note how the system flowchart graphically illustrates the physical system. Note how each symbol defines, at a black box level, one of the discrete components that make up this system. Note also how the flowlines define the logical path through the system.

Generally, the path of flow through a system flowchart is from top to bottom. However, many analysts prefer a left to right flow; for example, we could start with the display symbol at the left of the page and the reorder report at the right, and align the two programs and the reorder tape horizontally across the page. It's basically a matter of personal choice.

We have labeled each of the symbols in Fig. F.3, thus providing documentation. Many analysts prefer to add more detailed notations to a system flow diagram; some even add a separate page of explanation.

The flowchart for a complex system can be quite large. The offpage connector symbol can be used to continue the flowchart on a subsequent page, but a multiple-page flowchart can be very difficult to read. When faced with a complex system, many analysts begin by drawing a high level flowchart outlining the key functions; on subsequent pages, each of these functions is exploded, one at a time, to the appropriate level of detail. In the inventory system, for example, a first flowchart might show only three symbols: an inventory process, a report generation process, and the magnetic tape file that links them (Fig. F.4). A second page would then concentrate on the inventory process, showing (Fig. F.5) the CRT terminal, the inventory program, the disk master file, and the tape. Page three would explode the report generation process (Fig. F.6).

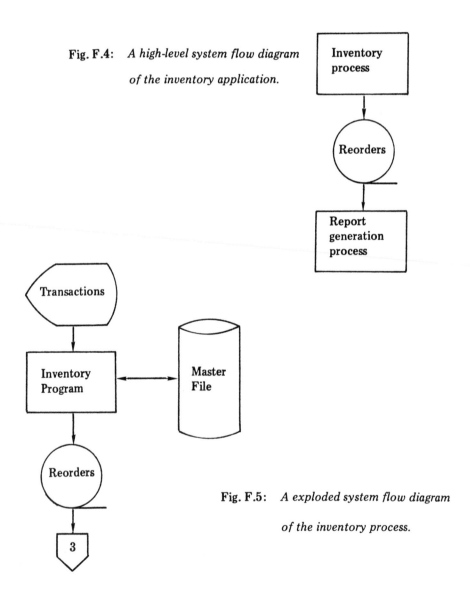

Fig. F.4:   *A high-level system flow diagram of the inventory application.*

Fig. F.5:   *A exploded system flow diagram of the inventory process.*

Fig. F.6: *An exploded system flow diagram*

of the report generation process.

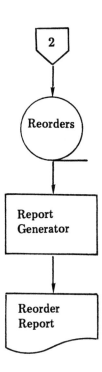

WHY USE SYSTEM FLOWCHARTS?

A data flow diagram presents a rather abstract picture of the system. In contrast, the system flowchart is more concrete. Specific programs or procedures replace the generalized processes, and specific files or data bases replace the data stores. Given the flowchart, it is possible to visualize how the system will be implemented. Such clear communication is particularly important at the end of the system design phase, when the user or management is asked to commit funds to implement the system.

The system flow diagram identifies each of the discrete components of the system. For planning purposes, these components can be attacked one at a time—the divide and conquer approach. Cost estimates are much more accurate when they are based on discrete, physical elements. A realistic implementation schedule can be devised, and parts of the work can be assigned to various groups in the organization. A system flow diagram is an excellent planning tool.

The further into the system life cycle we move, the more likely we are to encounter a group approach, with different people working independently on different aspects of the problem. A system flowchart represents a common reference point. By providing a visualization of the overall system, the system flowchart gives each independent group a sense of how their efforts fit into the bigger picture.

53

Fig. F.7: *A system flow diagram showing the hardware in a typical computer center.*

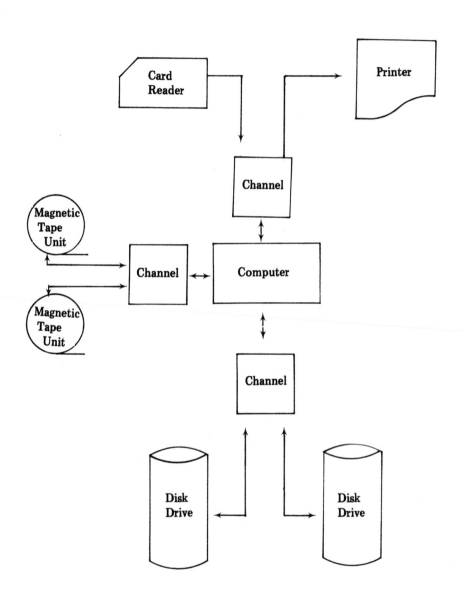

Some analysts use system flowcharts as a model to help develop job control language specifications. If IBM's job control language is used as an example, each program in the system calls for one EXEC statement, and each device or file that is linked to a program must be identified by a DD statement. A system flowchart clearly identifies each program and its associated input and output devices; thus each program symbol represents an EXEC statement and each file symbol implies a need for one DD statement. In effect, the system flowchart serves as a memory aid, helping the analyst to generate an accurate and complete set of job control statements.

OTHER USES

Often, the analyst must study the existing physical system. The objective is not to document the system fully, but to understand it. Too often, the documentation is unclear or incomplete. Drawing a flowchart is an excellent way to summarize a great deal of technical information and to highlight missing pieces.

A system flowchart can be used to map a hardware system (Fig. F.7); as an exercise, develop a flowchart showing the equipment in your school's computer center. Paperwork flows, procedural flows, and work flows can be described, too. Any time the analyst must summarize a number of physical facts concerning a system, a system flowchart might prove useful.

SYSTEM FLOWCHARTS AND DATABASES

The discrete, physical files tend to disappear on a database system. Rather than accessing a number of independent files to find information, a program accesses a central database; in effect, most online files are merged into that database. As a result, system flowcharts are somewhat less useful than they are when traditional files are used. Still, a system flowchart can provide a clear overview of a database application, showing key programs, data sources, and data destinations surrounding the database.

REFERENCES

1. Bohl, Marilyn (1978). *Tools for Structured Design.* Chicago: SRA.

2. Gore, Marvin and Stubbe (1979). *Elements of Systems Analysis for Business Data Processing, second edition.* Dubuque, Iowa: Wm. C. Brown Company Publishers.

3. Semprevivo, Philip C. (1982). *Systems Analysis: Definition, Process, and Design, second edition.* Chicago: SRA.

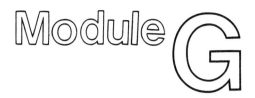

Cost/Benefit Analysis

COST/BENEFIT ANALYSIS

There is a difference between spending and investing. We spend money to get what we need today. We invest money because we hope to get even more at some point in the future. Developing a system is an investment. Funds must be committed throughout the system life cycle. In return, certain future benefits are expected, often in the form of reduced operating costs, or new revenues. If the expected benefits are not greater than the cost, then that system is not worth doing.

Management has numerous alternatives for investing an organization's money. One option is to loan it to someone else through a bank or a money market. The advantage of this approach is a limited risk; for example, when you deposit funds in a bank, you are confident that, at the end of a specified period of time, you will get your money back with interest. Investing that same amount of money in the development of a new system carries a risk. The cost might be higher than anticipated, and the benefits less than expected. Is the system a good investment? Cost/benefit analysis anwers this question by giving management a reasonable picture of the costs, benefits, and risks associated with a given system, so they can compare this investment alternative with others.

COSTS AND BENEFITS

To compare costs and benefits, the analyst must first estimate them. Let's begin with the cost of developing the system. Each phase in the system life cycle has a cost. In estimating the total cost of a given step, the analyst should consider personnel, equipment, supplies, overhead, and such external factors as consulting fees; a list of specific cost elements that might be considered is shown in Fig. G.1.

Once a system is implemented, the organization must begin paying continuing operating costs (Fig. G.2). A cost is associated with using the hardware. Equipment must be maintained. Operators must be paid to run the system; clerks use the system; programmers maintain the code. Supplies are consumed. Overhead must be supported. What is the difference between a development cost and an operating cost? Development costs occur once. When the system is released, development ceases; at this point, operating costs begin, and continue over the entire life of the system. The development cost is a capital investment; operating costs are expenses.

When individuals invest their time or money, they expect something in return—a benefit. Note that the payoff need not be financial; for example, to many people, education is its own reward. In a business environment, however, the objective is usually to make a profit, and thus an ideal return on investment (or benefit) is an increase in profit. Consider the basic profit equation:

$$PROFIT = REVENUE - COST$$

Revenue is money flowing into the organization; for example, receipts from sales. Cost is money flowing from the organization; for example, salaries, material expenses, and rent. There are two ways to increase profit: increase revenue or decrease cost.

Fig. G.1: *A checklist of typical development cost elements.*

Personnel
  Analysts
    Interviewing
    Preparation of reports
    Documentation
    Contemplation
    Preparation of procedures
    System test
    Inspections, walkthroughs
    Training — operators
    Training — clerical people
    Consultations — users
    Consultations — programmers
    Supervision — pilot operation
    Supervision — file conversion
    Forms design
    Formal presentations

  Programmers
    Coding
    Documentation
    Debug
    Inspections, walkthroughs
    Customizing purchased pgms.
    Consultations — analyst
    Consultations — programmers
    Formal presentations

  Operators
    Conversion
    Training
    Programmer support
    Consultations — analyst

  Clerical personnel
    Conversion
    Training
    Consultations — analysts

  Management
    Supervision
    Consultation — analyst

  Other
    Keypunching
    Data entry
    Art — forms design
    Technical writer — documentation

Equipment
  Capital expenditures
    New equipment
    Packaged software
  Equipment installation
  Equipment test and debug
  Existing equipment use
    Test and debug time
    Disk space
    Tapes
    Other supplies
  File conversion
  System test

Materials and Supplies
  Publication of procedures
  Paper, forms, cards
  Preparation — new forms
  Copies

Overhead
  Management support
  Secretarial support
  Heat, light, space

External
  Consulting fees
  Special training

Fig. G.2: *A checklist of typical operating cost elements.*

Hardware costs
   Computer residency time
   Main memory space
   I/O operations
   Secondary storage space
   Maintenance

Personnel costs
   Operator support
   Clerical support
   Programmers—maintenance
   Direct management support

Materials
   Forms
   Paper, cards
   Tapes
   Disk packs
   Scrap
   Inventory carrying cost

Overhead

External costs
   Leases
   Rentals
   Subcontracting
   Auditing

Thus a cost/benefit analysis will generally focus on either cost reduction or revenue enhancement.

Revenue might be increased through a new or improved product that leads to more sales; thus benefits are computed by subtracting the operating costs associated with achieving new sales from this new revenue. when cost reduction is the justification for the system, benefits are derived from the difference between the operating costs of the old and the new systems. Generally, the cost of an existing system is well documented in various accounting reports. However, expected new revenue or the cost of a new, not yet implemented system must be estimated, and any estimate is subject to error. This potential for error is a risk. A well-done cost/benefit analysis will clearly identify the estimated costs, benefits, and risks.

PERFORMING A COST/BENEFIT ANALYSIS

The first step in performing a cost benefit analysis is to estimate the development cost, the operating cost, and the benefits associated with the proposed system. The benefits and operating costs occur over the entire life of the system; how long should this life be? On a research and development project, the finished system might not even begin returning benefits for several years, so an expected life of ten years or more is common. The longer the life of a system, however, the greater the risk of obsolescence, so estimates of benefits and costs for a time far in the future are risky. We'll use a system life of five years for the examples that follow.

For example, consider a proposal for modifying an inventory system to generate a daily list of parts to be reordered by purchasing. Assume that the user and the analyst, working together, have estimated that the proposed system could save $2500 per year by reducing the risk of inventory shortages. Since the benefits are realized every year, it is convenient to show them in the form of a table (Fig. G.3). If the system is to be implemented, the inventory program will have to be modified to flag items to be reordered, and a new program will be needed to generate the reorder report; the analyst has estimated the cost of developing this system at $5000. We'll use these numbers to illustrate a cost/benefit analysis.

Fig. G.3:   *The cost and benefits of the inventory system.*

Development cost: $5000

Benefits:

Year	Amount
1	$2500
2	2500
3	2500
4	2500
5	2500

The Time Value of Money

How much would you be willing to invest today, to get $2500 in a year? If you think about it, the answer must be less than $2500. How much would you invest today to get $2500 in 5 years? Even less! $2500 today, $2500 a year from now, and $2500 in five years are not the same. Money has time value. Comparing present dollars to future dollars is a bit like comparing apples and oranges.

The time value of money is often expressed in the form of interest. A simple formula can be used to compute the future value of an investment assuming compound interest:

$$F = P (1+i)^n$$

where:

P is the present value of the investment,
F is the future value of an investment,
P is the present value of the investment,
i is the interest rate per compounding period,
n is the number of compounding periods (usually years).

For example, if $5000 is invested in a certificate of deposit for 3 years at 12 percent interest, the value of that $5000 at the end of the 3 years would be:

61

$$F = 5000 (1+0.12)^3 = 5000 (1.12)^3 = 7024.64$$

Look again at Fig. G.3. We have an investment of $5000. Benefits are estimated at $2500 per year. The investment must be made "this year"; in other words, we have its present value. The benefits, however, occur in the future, and we cannot compare present values to future values without considering the time value of the money. Think, for example, of the $2500 we expect to receive at the end of the fifth year. How much would you be willing to invest right now, at current interest rates, to get $2500 at the end of 5 years? The answer is the present value of the benefit, which can be compared to the present value of the investment.

How do we compute the present value of the benefits? Start with the basic compound interest formula:

$$F = P (1+i)^n$$

Solve this equation for P, the present value:

$$P = \frac{F}{(1+i)^n}$$

Using this equation, we can compute the present value of a $2500 benefit 5 years from now (assuming 12 percent interest) as:

$$P = \frac{2500}{(1+0.12)^5} = 1418.57$$

In other words, if we invest $1418.57 today at 12 percent interest, we can expect to withdraw $2500 after 5 years. Converting a future value to its present value equivalent is known as discounting.

This computation can be repeated for each year's expected benefit; the answers are summarized in Fig. G.4. We now have the present values of both the investment and the benefits, and can begin comparing them.

An interest rate of 12 percent was used above, purely for illustration. In practice, the interest rate used to discount future values should reflect a realistic, low-risk investment option. If a local bank is paying 14 percent on guaranteed certificates of deposit, 14 percent might be an excellent choice. Many business organizations use the widely publicized prime rate; a large company can always invest its money at or near this rate with little risk. Developing a new system is risky. If the proposed system does not promise a higher return, then the low-risk, "sure thing" is a better investment.

Fig. G.4:   *The present values and accumulated present values of the annual benefits.*

Year	Future value	$(1+i)^n$	Present value	Cumulative Present value
1	2500	1.12	2234.14	2234.14
2	2500	1.25	1992.98	4225.12
3	2500	1.40	1779.45	6004.57
4	2500	1.57	1588.80	7593.37
5	2500	1.76	1418.57	9011.94

The Payback Period

One common measure of the relative value of a project is its payback period: How long does it take for the accumulated benefits to equal the initial investment? Obviously, the shorter this payback period, the sooner we begin realizing a profit; thus, the more desirable the investment becomes.

Look, for example, at Fig. G.4; the last column on the right shows the cumulative present values of the benefits. The investment is $5000. At the end of the first year, the accumulated present value of the benefits (only one year) is $2234.14, not nearly enough to offset the initial investment. At the end of the second year, the accumulated present value of the benefits amounts to $4225.12; still not enough to cover the investment. By the end of the third year, however, the accumulated benefits come to $6004.57; thus payback occurs somewhere in the third year. After two full years, we had $4225.12 in benefits. We need $5000 to reach payback; the difference is $774.88. The present value of the third year's benefits is $1779.45; thus we need 44 percent of that third year's benefits. The payback period is 2.44 years.

The payback period is a very conservative economic measure; it should not be used alone. It is, however, quite valuable when used in combination with other measures, particularly when the risk of technological obsolescence is significant.

The Net Present Value

Another useful measure is net present value: the difference between the present value of the benefits and the present value of the investment. The inventory application (Fig. G.4), for example, yields a cumulative benefit of $9011.94 on an investment of $5000; that's a net present value of $4011.94. Earlier, future benefits were discounted back to their present values using a simple formula; in our example, we assumed a 12 percent interest rate. The net present value can be viewed as the amount of benefit over what could have been earned on an imaginary, risk-free investment. If the net present value is zero, the project will return the same amount as that risk-free investment, and thus is probably not worth doing. If the net present value is negative, the project is definitely not worth doing, as the imaginary risk-free investment would earn more.

In an effort to compare alternative investment opportunities, the net present value is sometimes expressed as a percentage of the investment, for example:

$$\frac{4013.94}{5000.00} = 0.80 \text{ or } 80\%$$

Given the 5 year life of the project, this number might be restated as 16 percent per year. Be careful in using such statistics, however; that 16 percent figure cannot be compared with the annual percentage rates offered by a bank or paid on a loan. The number does provide a relative measure of a project's return on investment, and can prove useful in comparing alternatives as long as the "rate of return" is computed in the same way, but it is not an absolute measure of the project's true return on investment.

The Internal Rate of Return

It is possible to compute an internal rate of return that can be compared with the prime rate and other common financial market statistics. To do this, we treat the interest rate as an unknown. We have the present value of the investment, and a series of estimated future benefits. Imagine that we were to place the initial investment in a savings account, and withdraw the appropriate estimated future value at the end of each year; for example, in the inventory problem, we would deposit $5000 now, and withdraw $2500 each year for 5 years. At the end of the time period, there would be nothing left in the account. What interest rate would we have to earn to be able to make this pattern of withdrawals and have nothing left after 5 years?

The key to solving the problem is the fact that, at the end of the specified time period, nothing is left. Thus, as long as the point in time is consistent, the investment and the benefits must be equal. Choosing the present as our common time period, we can write the following equation:

$$P = F_1 \left[\frac{1}{(1+i)^1} \right] + F_2 \left[\frac{1}{(1+i)^2} \right] + F_3 \left[\frac{1}{(1+i)^3} \right] + \ldots + F_n \left[\frac{1}{(1+i)^n} \right]$$

Rearranging the terms, we get:

$$0 = -P + F_1 \left[\frac{1}{(1+i)^1} \right] + F_2 \left[\frac{1}{(1+i)^2} \right] + F_3 \left[\frac{1}{(1+i)^3} \right] + \ldots + F_n \left[\frac{1}{(1+i)^n} \right]$$

64

which is a polynomial. Many scientific subroutines are available to solve polynomials, and many programmable calculators offer a polynomial routine. Figure G.5 shows a simple BASIC program that estimates, to the nearest full percentage point, the internal rate of return for a project with a 5 year life; you may want to generalize this program. It should be noted that other techniques might be used to generate more accurate results, or to iterate to a solution in fewer steps; this program is presented because of its simplicity.

The internal rate of return is analogous to the annual percentage rate, the number that banks and financial institutions use when advertising an investment opportunity or a loan; thus it is possible to use this number to compare or to rank alternatives both inside and outside the organization. For this reason, it is the preferred measure in any cost/benefit analysis. The internal rate of return for the inventory problem (as estimated by the program of Fig. G.5) lies between 41 and 42 percent (Fig. G.6).

RISK

Consider three different investment alternatives: a bank deposit, a new inventory system, or the fourth horse in the third race. The bank is virtually a sure thing. The inventory system may seem very straightforward, but estimates of cost and benefit can be wrong, and if they are, the rate of return will be wrong; thus an element of risk is involved. The horse race is a pure gamble, no matter how good your inside information may be. It is possible that the computed rate of return for all three alternatives could be the same, but the degree of risk is quite different. An investor expects to be compensated for risk; the greater the risk, the higher the rate of return that will be required.

The analyst must communicate risk to management. One common technique is to provide an optimistic estimate, a pessimistic estimate, and a most likely estimate for each questionable cost or benefit. Often, these three estimates are weighted: 20 percent, 20 percent, and 60 percent (for the most likely), and the result of this weighting process is used in all cost/benefit computations. Another option is to perform a complete cost/benefit analysis using only the worst case numbers (maximum cost and minimum benefit); the actual outcome is not likely to be any worse. Given a reasonable assessment of the risk, management can make an intelligent decision.

ESTIMATING COSTS

In discussing cost/benefit analysis, we have essentially treated the cost and benefit estimates as given. We presented two checklists of typical cost factors (Figs. G.1 an G.2), but said little about how the analyst might use this information to estimate costs. An in-depth treatment of cost estimating is well beyond the scope of this book, but we can present a number of general guidelines.

It is difficult to estimate the cost of a system. It is much easier to estimate the costs of each of the system components, and then sum these results; the total cost of the system is, after all, nothing more than the sum of the costs of its parts. Thus, the first step in developing a cost estimate is to break the problem into as many pieces as possible. During the feasibility study, this subdivision might be limited to the steps in

Fig. G.5: *A BASIC program to estimate the internal rate of return.*

```
10                        REM  * * * * * * * * * * * * * * * *
20                        REM  * Program to compute the internal    *
30                        REM  * rate of return for a project with a *
40                        REM  * five year expected life.           *
50                        REM  *    By:   W.S. Davis                 *
60                        REM  *          1/15/83                    *
70                        REM  * Variables:                         *
80                        REM  *   F  =   future value, benefits     *
90                        REM  *   P  =   present value, investment  *
100                       REM  *   X  =   net present value          *
110                       REM  *   N  =   year (maximum of 5)        *
120                       REM  * * * * * * * * * * * * * * * *
130   DIM  F(5)
140   PRINT "Enter initial investment amount";
150   INPUT P
160   FOR N = 1 TO 5
170      PRINT "Enter benefit amount for year   ";N;
180      INPUT F(N)
190   NEXT N
200                       REM  * * * * * * * * * * * * * * * *
210                       REM  * Once all the data have been        *
220                       REM  * entered, compute net present value.*
230                       REM  * If it is negative, the investment is *
240                       REM  * larger than the sum of the benefits, *
250                       REM  * and there is no return on invest-   *
260                       REM  * ment.                               *
270                       REM  * * * * * * * * * * * * * * * *
280   LET  X = F(1)+F(2)+F(3)+F(4)+F(5)-P ,
290   IF X > = 0 THEN 420
300   PRINT  "The amount of the investment is greater than or equal to"
310   PRINT  "the sum of the benefits. There is no return."
320   STOP
330                       REM  * * * * * * * * * * * * * * * *
340                       REM  * If the net present value is positive, *
350                       REM  * the value of the polynomial is      *
360                       REM  * computed with a 1% rate. The        *
370                       REM  * value is then re-computed for       *
380                       REM  * increments of 1% until the net      *
390                       REM  * present value becomes negative or   *
400                       REM  * zero.                               *
410                       REM  * * * * * * * * * * * * * * * *
420   FOR I = .01 TO 1 STEP .01
430      LET X = (-P)
440      FOR N = 1 TO 5
450         LET X = X + F(N) / (1+I) ↑ N
460      NEXT N
470      IF X < = 0 THEN 580
480   NEXT I
490   PRINT "The rate of return exceeds 100%."
500   STOP
510                       REM  * * * * * * * * * * * * * * * *
520                       REM  * The internal rate of return is less *
530                       REM  * than or equal to the rate that      *
540                       REM  * caused the net present value to      *
550                       REM  * become negative or zero. Thus,       *
560                       REM  * both (I-0.01) and I are printed.     *
570                       REM  * * * * * * * * * * * * * * * *
580   PRINT "The internal rate of return lies between:"
590   PRINT I-.01; "or"; (I-.01)*100; "percent; and"
600   PRINT I; "or"; I*100; "percent"
610   END
```

66

```
Enter initial investment amount?  5000
Enter benefit amount for year  1  ?  2500
Enter benefit amount for year  2  ?  2500
Enter benefit amount for year  3  ?  2500
Enter benefit amount for year  4  ?  2500
Enter benefit amount for year  5  ?  2500
The internal rate of return lies between:
  .4099999 or 40.99999 percent; and
  .4199999 or 41.99999 percent
```

the system life cycle, yielding an estimate that is perhaps accurate to ±50 percent. Later, the personnel, equipment, and material costs associated with each step might be estimated separately. During detailed design those personnel costs might be subdivided into programmers, operators, clerks, and others. Eventually, the analyst may be able to break the work of the programmers down to individual modules on a hierarchy chart, and generate a much more accurate cost estimate; the smaller the module, the easier it is to estimate the cost.

On most systems, the bulk of the cost is concentrated in a few of the system components. By evaluating these few key elements carefully, it is possible to develop a very accurate cost estimate with a minimum of effort. If the handful of factors that account for 80 or even 90 percent of a system's cost can be identified and accurately estimated, ballpark figures or even guesses may be perfectly adequate for the other factors.

Historical data are an important source of information. Try to find the actual expenses for a past project of similar scope; they can provide a very good set of guidelines or targets. Of course, the actual cost of the existing system (as recorded by accounting) is the standard against which the new system is measured, and can prove invaluable in estimating the cost of a new system. Consider also the inspection process as described in Module A. As part of that process, rework time is estimated; later the actual rework time is recorded. If properly maintained, such data can be extremely useful.

Standards provide another source of cost information. Many firms add a fixed percentage to the sum of all other costs to cover overhead. Maintenance might be estimated as a fixed percentage of the implementation cost. We might use a number like 10 percent of programmer cost to estimate computer charges during the program test and debug period.

Personnel costs are a function of time; thus if we can estimate the time required to do a job, we can often estimate its cost. Let's assume that, based on historical data, our programmers average 10 lines of tested, documented, debugged code per day.

Given this standard, a good way to estimate the cost of a program is to start with the hierarchy chart. Each block represents one module, and each module should be limited to roughly one page of code—about 50 lines. That's an average of five programmer days per module; a moderate program containing 50 modules would be expected to take roughly 250 days. If programmers cost $100 per day, that's $25,000. Rather than using an average of five days per module, the analyst could, of course, evaluate each module independently, and thus develop more accurate estimates; the sum of these estimates would then represent the total time needed to write the program. Most organizations have standard personnel costs, and many have established coding standards based on measures such as lines of code per day.

When you prepare a cost estimate, remember to break the system into pieces first. Estimate the cost of each piece separately; to get the system cost, sum the components that represent the bulk of the system cost. Take advantage of historical cost figures and standards whenever possible. Cost estimating is not easy, but with a little work you can learn to do a good job.

REFERENCES

1. Teichroew, D. (1964). *An Introduction to Management Science*. New York: John Wiley and Sons, Inc.

2. Numerous books are available on such topics as engineering economic analysis, business economic analysis, management science, and investment analysis. Most contain at least a chapter or two on cost/benefit analysis.

HIPO with Structured English

WITH: *Laurena Burk*

THE HIPO TECHNIQUE

Once we have completed the analysis stage of the system life cycle, we should have a logical module of the system documented by a data flow diagram, a data dictionary, and a description of key algorithms. During system design, a system flowchart may be created; it typically identifies, at a black box level, one or more programs. In this module, we will develop a set of specifications for those programs using the *HIPO (Hierarchy plus Input/Process/Output)* technique.

A completed HIPO package has two parts. A *hierarchy chart* is used to represent the top down structure of the program. For each module depicted on the hierarchy chart, an *IPO (Input/Process/Output) chart* is used to describe the inputs to, the outputs from, and the process performed by the module; the data dictionary is the source of the inputs and outputs, and the algorithm descriptions define the processes.

The HIPO documentation serves a number of purposes. By using it, designers can evaluate and refine a design, and correct flaws prior to implementation. Given the graphic nature of HIPO, users and managers can easily follow a program's structure. Finally, programmers can use the hierarchy and IPO charts as they write, maintain, or modify the program.

AN EXAMPLE

In Module F, we developed a system flowchart for an inventory application. The flowchart identified two programs; we'll use the HIPO technique to prepare specifications for the inventory update program. What basic functions are necessary to update the inventory master file? We might begin by listing the following major steps:

1. Get a transaction.

2. Get the master record.

3. Process the transaction.

4. Rewrite the master record.

5. Write a reorder record (if necessary).

We can summarize these steps in a high-level hierarchy chart (Fig. H.1). At the top is the main control module, *Update Inventory*, which controls the order in which the lower level modules are invoked. *Get Transaction* is the first subordinate module to be called, followed by *Get Inventory, Process Transaction, Rewrite Inventory,* and *Write Reorder*. As each subordinate module completes its task, control is passed back to the main control module, which invokes the next subordinate module. The arrangement of modules graphically represents the program hierarchy.

Note the names chosen for the modules. Each consists of a strong verb followed by a clear subject. The name tells you what the module does, and thus adds to the documentation.

Fig. H.1: *The first-level hierarchy of the on-line inventory update program.*

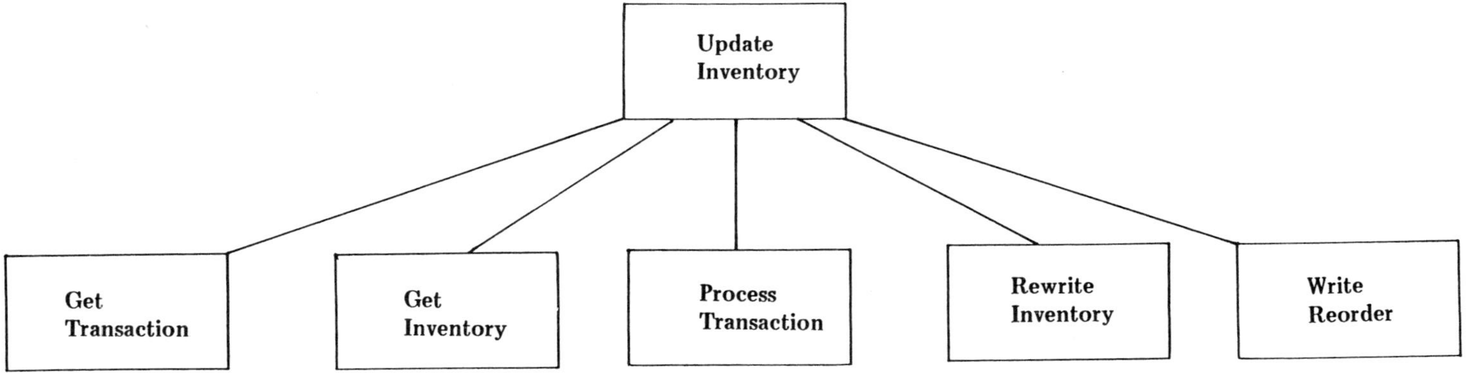

A separate IPO chart supports each module on the hierarchy chart (see Figs. H.2 through H.6). For example, consider the IPO chart for Get Inventory (Fig. H.3). The top lines on the chart identify the system, the module, and the author. Next, we show how this module is related to other modules: *Get Inventory* is called by *Update Inventory*, and calls no lower level modules. The part number and an error flag flow into *Get Inventory* from *Update Inventory*; the inventory record and the error flag flow back to *Update Inventory*. The logic performed by *Get Inventory* is clearly identified in the process block. Finally, there is space near the bottom of the chart for a list of local data elements and notes.

Many sources use a more elaborate IPO chart than the one described in this module. Often, large arrows are used to illustrate data flows graphically. Our intent is to concentrate on the essence of the HIPO technique, however, and we can do this with a minimum of detail. Another advantage to our simplified IPO diagrams is ease of maintenance, a topic we will return to later.

Fig. H.2: *An IPO chart for the Get Transaction module.*

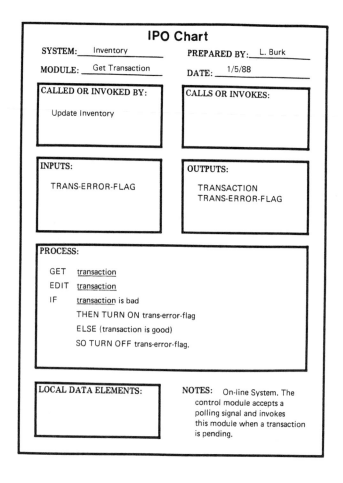

72

Fig. H.3: *The Get Master IPO chart.*

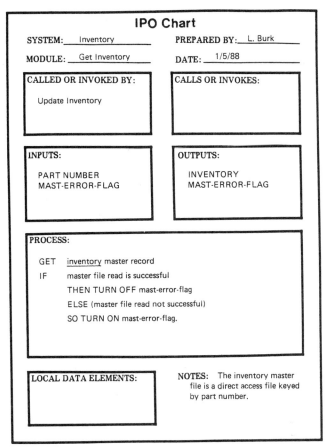

Functional Decomposition

A hierarchy chart is developed from the top, down. High level modules are general, performing control functions, while detailed computations are normally performed at the lower levels. Should we break any of the modules shown in Fig. H.1 down to a lower level? Ideally, each module should perform a single, complete logical function. Consider, for example, *Process Transaction*. What functions make up this module? Basically, we might consider four transaction types:

1. Increase the stock on hand as items are received at the warehouse.

2. Decrease the stock on hand as items are shipped from the warehouse.

3. Add a new record to the inventory file.

4. Delete an old record from the inventory file.

73

Fig. H.5: The Rewrite Inventory IPO chart.

IPO Chart

SYSTEM: _Inventory_ PREPARED BY: _L. Burk_

MODULE: _Rewrite Inventory_ DATE: _1/5/88_

CALLED OR INVOKED BY:

Update Inventory

CALLS OR INVOKES:

INPUTS:

INVENTORY
REWRITE-ERROR-FLAG

OUTPUTS:

REWRITE-ERROR-FLAG

PROCESS:

REWRITE inventory master record.

IF rewrite is successful

THEN TURN OFF rewrite-error-flag

ELSE (rewrite is not successful)

SO TURN ON rewrite-error-flag.

LOCAL DATA ELEMENTS:

NOTES:

Fig. H.4: The Process Transaction IPO chart.

IPO Chart

SYSTEM: _Inventory_ PREPARED BY: _L. Burk_

MODULE: _Process Transaction_ DATE: _1/5/88_

CALLED OR INVOKED BY:

Update Inventory

CALLS OR INVOKES:

Increase Stock
Decrease Stock
Add Record
Delete Record

INPUTS:

TRANSACTION
INVENTORY

OUTPUTS:

INVENTORY (updated)
UPDATE-ERROR-FLAG

PROCESS:

IF increase stock transaction
  THEN DO Increase Stock.
IF decrease stock transaction
  THEN DO Decrease Stock.
IF add record transaction
  THEN DO Add Record.
IF delete record transaction
  THEN DO Delete Record.

LOCAL DATA ELEMENTS:

NOTES:

Fig. H.6: *The Write Reorder IPO chart.*

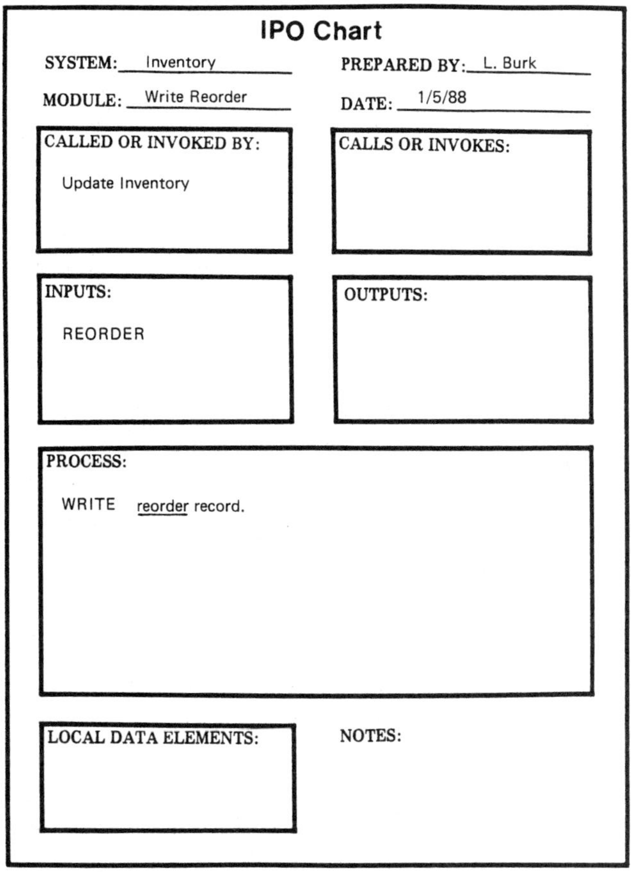

IPO Chart

SYSTEM: ___Inventory___   PREPARED BY: __L. Burk__

MODULE: __Write Reorder__   DATE: __1/5/88__

CALLED OR INVOKED BY:	CALLS OR INVOKES:
Update Inventory	

INPUTS:	OUTPUTS:
REORDER	

PROCESS:

WRITE   reorder record.

LOCAL DATA ELEMENTS:	NOTES:

Processing transactions to update the inventory master file requires four different algorithms, one for each transaction type. A given transaction will call for only one of these algorithms. Each transaction type, each algorithm, represents an independent function; thus the *Process Transaction* module should be subdivided into four lower level modules (Fig. H.7). Breaking a module into its subtasks is called *functional decomposition.* A module that performs a single, complete logical function is said to be *cohesive.*

Should any of these modules be further decomposed? Consider *Increase Stock*; its IPO chart is shown in Fig. H.8. The process block identifies only a single function—calculate stock on hand. Since the module performs a single, complete logical function, it is already cohesive, and further decomposition is unnecessary.

75

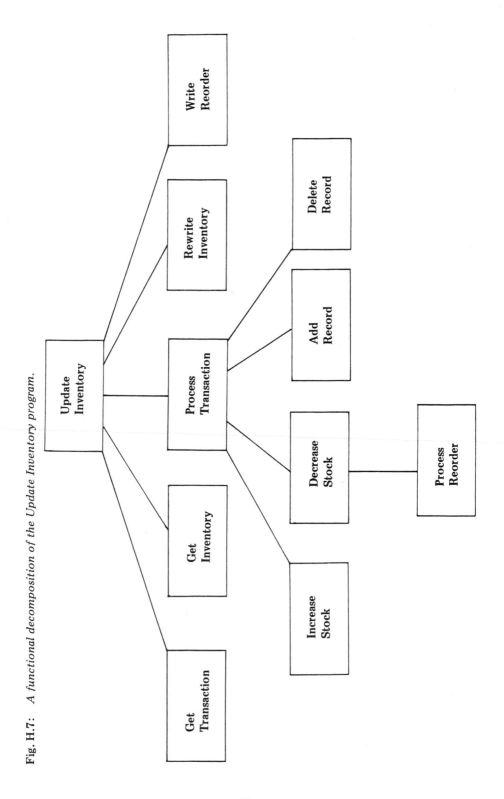

Fig. H.7: *A functional decomposition of the Update Inventory program.*

Next, consider *Decrease Stock* (Fig. H.9). Two functions can be identified; we always calculate stock-on-hand, but sometimes find it necessary to process a reorder as well. It might be reasonable to define *Process Reorder* as a subtask of *Decrease Stock* (Fig. H.7).

Is cohesion enough? Not really. It might be argued that *Process Transaction* is a complete logical function, and thus should not be decomposed. Without decomposition, however, *Process Transaction* would be so large that it would be difficult to follow. As a rule, no module should exceed a single page of code; as a planning guideline, decompose a module when its process cannot be completely defined on a single IPO chart. A well designed program is composed of a hierarchy of small, cohesive modules.

In the interest of brevity, we will not decompose the other modules of Fig. H.7.

Fig. H.8: *The Increase Stock IPO chart.*

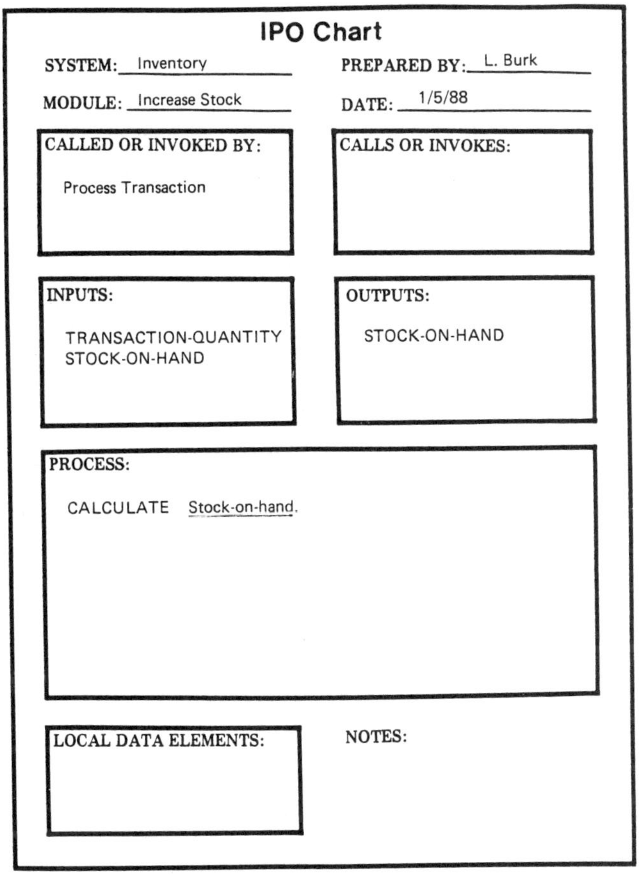

IPO Chart

SYSTEM: Inventory   PREPARED BY: L. Burk

MODULE: Increase Stock   DATE: 1/5/88

CALLED OR INVOKED BY:

Process Transaction

CALLS OR INVOKES:

INPUTS:

TRANSACTION-QUANTITY
STOCK-ON-HAND

OUTPUTS:

STOCK-ON-HAND

PROCESS:

CALCULATE Stock-on-hand.

LOCAL DATA ELEMENTS: NOTES:

Fig. H.9:   *The Decrease Stock IPO chart.*

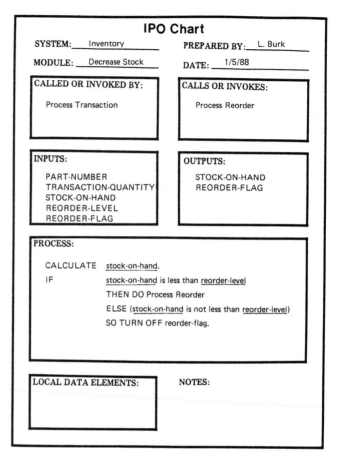

IPO Chart

SYSTEM:____Inventory_____   PREPARED BY:___L. Burk_____

MODULE: ___Decrease Stock_____   DATE: ____1/5/88_____

CALLED OR INVOKED BY:

Process Transaction

CALLS OR INVOKES:

Process Reorder

INPUTS:

    PART-NUMBER
    TRANSACTION-QUANTITY
    STOCK-ON-HAND
    REORDER-LEVEL
    REORDER-FLAG

OUTPUTS:

    STOCK-ON-HAND
    REORDER-FLAG

PROCESS:

    CALCULATE   stock-on-hand.
    IF   stock-on-hand is less than reorder-level
                    THEN DO Process Reorder
                    ELSE (stock-on-hand is not less than reorder-level)
                    SO TURN OFF reorder-flag.

LOCAL DATA ELEMENTS: NOTES:

Checking the Flow of Control

Once we have created the functionally decomposed hierarchy chart, we must review the flow of control through the program. Control normally flows from the top, down, following the lines that link the modules. The scope of control of a given module extends only over those modules lower in the hierarchy chart; a low-level module never tells its parent what to do. In Fig. H.7, for example, *Process Transaction* should control only itself and its subordinates. *Update Inventory* may tell *Rewrite Inventory* what to do, but *Process Transaction* may not. The analyst should carefully check the processes on each IPO chart to make sure that the rules concerning the flow of control have not been violated. Since the modules are ultimately linked by data flows, the next step is to check for data independence.

Data Coupling and Data Independence

We know that data must pass between modules; thus relationships among the modules are essential. What data should be allowed to flow into a module? Only those elements

78

that are essential to the module's function. What data should flow out from a module? Once again, only essential data should move. Why? One reason is ease of maintenance. If a data element is altered in form, then every module that accesses that data element is a candidate for maintenance. Why maintain a module just because a nonessential data element changes? Why waste time? Another problem, the ripple effect, occurs when a bug in one module propagates bugs in other modules. Modules are linked by data flows. An unnecessary data flow represents an unnecessary risk. Finally, consider program simplicity. What is easier to understand, a subroutine with a parameter list of three elements, or one with six? Unnecessary data flows mean unnecessary complexity.

Data coupling is a measure of the links between modules. The more loosely modules are coupled, the more independent they are. We achieve module independence and reduce data coupling by minimizing the number of connections, or the number of data flows, linking a module to the rest of the program. The IPO chart lists the data links in the input and output blocks; thus we must study the IPO charts to be sure that coupling is loose, by verifying that all input to a module is essential to its function, and that no superfluous data are passed to or returned by a module.

The Structure Chart

Following data from IPO to IPO is difficult. An excellent way to keep track of the data flows is to develop a *structure chart*. Start with a single IPO chart. Locate the module associated with this IPO on the hierarchy chart, and copy each of the input and output data element names alongside the line linking this module to its parent. Use small arrows to indicate the direction of flow: into the module or back to the higher level. Repeat this process for each IPO chart, and you have a structure chart (Fig. H.10). (Note that two new IPO charts, Figs. H.11 and H.12, have been added to the six presented earlier in the chapter.)

Given a structure chart, we can easily evaluate data coupling. Remember the key rule: only those data elements that are required by a module should be passed to that module. Note that two structures flow into *Process Transaction*. (Remember that a structure contains a number of data elements). Are all data elements contained in both the inventory and transaction structures needed by *Process Transaction*, or by a module controlled by *Process Transaction*? Yes. Consider, for example, *Add Record* (Fig. H.12). The only way to add a complete record to the inventory file is to have a complete record; the only way *Add Record* can get a complete record is if *Process Transaction* passes it a complete record.

In contrast, note *Increase Stock* (Fig. H.8). Why are only selected data elements sent to this module? Does *Increase Stock* need every element in both the transaction and the inventory records? No. Since *Increase Stock* does not need such data elements as the part number, part description, and reorder quantity, there is no need to pass these elements to *Increase Stock*. Generally, a program should be designed to keep entire data structures in management modules, and to pass to the subordinate modules only those elements essential to their function. Structures are helpful in grouping related fields, but bundling data just to shorten a parameter list leads to confusion, and not simplification.

79

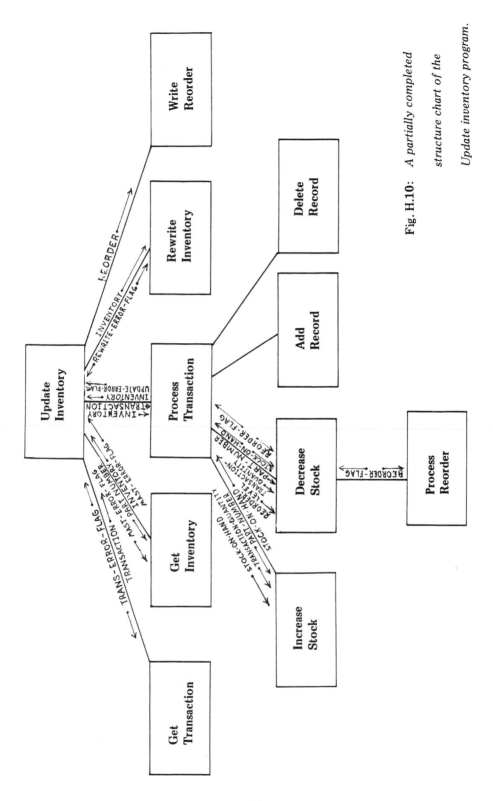

Fig. H.10: *A partially completed structure chart of the Update inventory program.*

For documentation purposes, adding data flows to a hierarchy chart is probably counterproductive: a structure chart is hard to maintain and difficult to read. A structure chart should be used to verify a design. Take the time to review each module in the HIPO, and make sure that it is independent and loosely coupled.

STRUCTURED ENGLISH

In this module, we have used *structured English* to define the process steps on each IPO chart. Structured English is a very limited, highly restricted subset of the English language. In some ways, it resembles a programming language; thus programmers tend to find it easy to understand. The base for structured English is, of course, English, so users find it easy to follow, too.

Fig. H.11: *The Process Reorder IPO chart.*

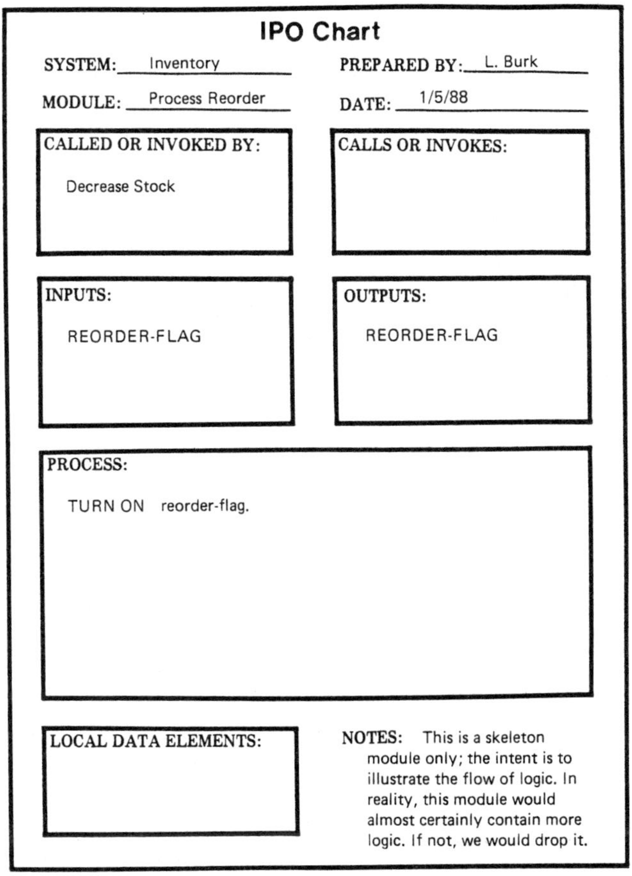

<table>
<tr><td colspan="2" align="center">IPO Chart</td></tr>
<tr><td>SYSTEM: Inventory</td><td>PREPARED BY: L. Burk</td></tr>
<tr><td>MODULE: Process Reorder</td><td>DATE: 1/5/88</td></tr>
<tr><td>CALLED OR INVOKED BY:

Decrease Stock</td><td>CALLS OR INVOKES:</td></tr>
<tr><td>INPUTS:

REORDER-FLAG</td><td>OUTPUTS:

REORDER-FLAG</td></tr>
<tr><td colspan="2">PROCESS:

TURN ON reorder-flag.</td></tr>
<tr><td>LOCAL DATA ELEMENTS:</td><td>NOTES: This is a skeleton module only; the intent is to illustrate the flow of logic. In reality, this module would almost certainly contain more logic. If not, we would drop it.</td></tr>
</table>

81

Fig. H.12: *The Add Record IPO chart.*

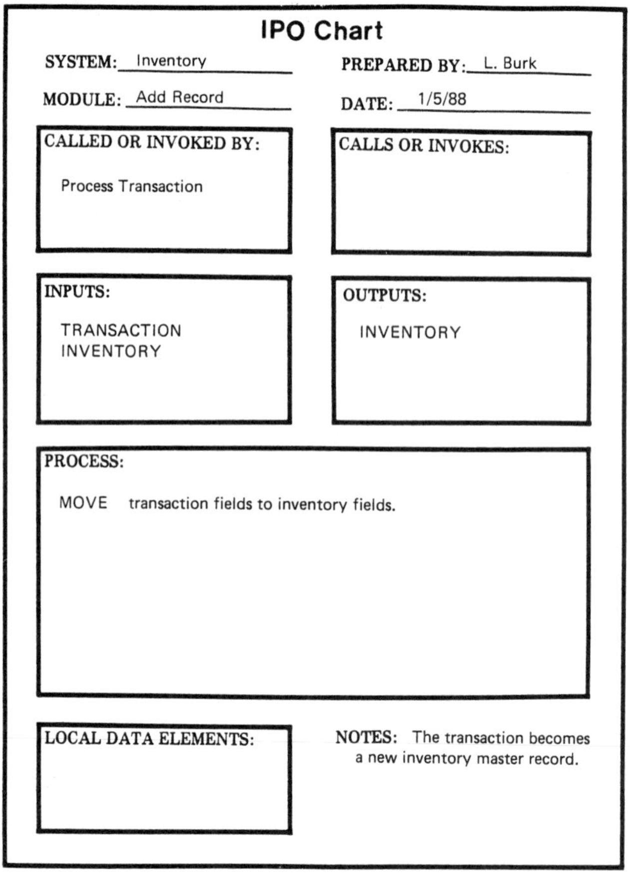

IPO Chart

SYSTEM: Inventory   PREPARED BY: L. Burk

MODULE: Add Record   DATE: 1/5/88

CALLED OR INVOKED BY:

Process Transaction

CALLS OR INVOKES:

INPUTS:

TRANSACTION
INVENTORY

OUTPUTS:

INVENTORY

PROCESS:

MOVE   transaction fields to inventory fields.

LOCAL DATA ELEMENTS:

NOTES: The transaction becomes
a new inventory master record.

There are several variations of structured English, and none even approaches the status of a standard; we can, however, offer a number of guidelines. Three basic instruction types are used: sequence, decision, and repetition. Sequence instructions are the simpliest; CALCULATE new stock-on-hand is a good one. Sequence statements begin with commands such as MOVE, GET, WRITE, READ, or COMPUTE, followed by the name or names of the associated data elements. A good structured English statement reads like a short imperative sentence; several examples are shown in Fig. H.13.

> COMPUTE <u>gross-pay</u>.
>
> ADD 1 to counter.
>
> MULTIPLY <u>hours-worked</u> by <u>pay-rate</u> to get <u>gross-pay</u>.
>
> GET <u>master-record</u>.
>
> MOVE <u>field-a</u> to <u>output-record</u>.
>
> WRITE new <u>master-record</u>.
>
> TURN ON reorder-flag.

It is often convenient to group several structured English statements into a block, assign a name to the block, and treat it as a single sequence statement. For example, all the instructions required to compute gross pay might be grouped in a block under the name *compute gross pay*. Once this has been done, we can write:

> DO *compute <u>gross pay</u>*.

and reference the entire block. Note that the gross pay logic might well contain decisions and even repetitive code; a block can contain any combination of code.

Decision logic follows the IF-THEN-ELSE structure. For example:

> IF <u>stock-on-hand</u> is less than <u>reorder-point</u>
>
> THEN turn on reorder-flag
>
> ELSE (<u>stock-on-hand</u> not less than <u>reorder-point</u>)
>
> SO turn off reorder-flag

The key word IF is followed by a condition. If the condition is true, the block following THEN is executed. ELSE identifies the negative of the condition; SO preceeds the block to be executed if the initial condition is false. In general write:

IF condition

    THEN block-1

    ELSE (not condition)

    SO block-2.

Indenting makes the IF-THEN-ELSE logic easier to read.

Earlier, we mentioned that a block of structured English code can contain any combination of sequence, decision, and repetition logic. Thus, in the general structure of the decision logic described above, block-1 or block-2 (or both) could contain another decision, for example:

    IF condition-1

        THEN IF condition-2

            THEN block-a

            ELSE (not condition-2)

            SO block-b

        ELSE (not condition-1)

        SO block-c.

This is a nested decision. Note that any or all of the three logic blocks could contain yet another decision.

Repetitive logic defines a block of structured English that is executed repeatedly until a terminal condition is reached. For example, such instructions as:

    REPEAT UNTIL condition-1

        block-1

    FOR EACH TRANSACTION

        block-a

imply both repetitive logic and the condition used to terminate that logic.

By convention, only key words such as IF, THEN, SO, REPEAT, UNTIL, DO, and so on are capitalized; data names and the general English needed to complete a sentence or a phrase should be lower case. Many sources recommend that a data name defined in a data dictionary be underlined. Indentation should always be used to show the relationship between the parts of a block.

Structured English is excellent for describing an algorithm, particularly when user communication is necessary. If the main concern is communication with the programmers, however, pseudocode may be a better choice (see Module I). Both tools are less effective at describing the logic of a high level control structure or an algorithm in which numerous decisions must be made. In these cases, a logic flowchart (Module J), a decision table, or a decision tree (Module O) may be a better choice. No single tool is always best. Choose the technique that best fits the application.

HIPO AND LONG-TERM DOCUMENTATION

Ideally, the hierarchy chart and the IPO charts should form the core of a long-term documentation package. As the program changes (and it will), the documentation should change, too. Unfortunately, this is not always the case. In this module, we have considered only the essence of the HIPO technique; most sources recommend a more elaborate procedure for developing the IPO charts, with large arrows graphically depicting the data flows. Unless an organization has professional documentators or a dependable, on-line, computer-aided documentation system, it is unlikely that such charts will be maintained for very long. A distinct advantage to the "essential elements only" approach of this module is the fact that an IPO chart can be imbedded into the source code as a series of comments. Source code comments are perhaps the easiest form of documentation to maintain.

REFERENCES

1. Gane, Chris and Sarson (1979). *Structured Systems Analysis: Tools and Techniques.* Englewood Cliffs, New Jersey: Prentice-Hall, Inc.

2. IBM Corporation (1974). *HIPO—A Design Aid and Documentation Technique.* White Plains, New York: IBM Corporation. Publication Number GC20-1851.

3. Katzan, Harry Jr. (1976). *Systems Design and Documentation: An Introduction to the HIPO Method.* New York: Van Nostrand Reinhold.

4. Peters, Lawrence J. (1981). *Software Design: Methods and Techniques.* New York: Yourdon Press.

5. Yourdon, Edward and Constantine (1979). *Structured Design.* Englewood Cliffs, New Jersey: Prentice-Hall, Inc.

Module

Pseudocode

WHAT IS PSEUDOCODE?

In Module H, structured English was used to describe the logic of a process on an IPO chart. Pseudocode is an alternative to structured English. *Pseudo-* means similar to; thus pseudocode is similar to real code. In fact, the structure of pseudocode is often based on a real programming language such as COBOL, FORTRAN, or Pascal. When structured English is used, such details as opening and closing files, initializing counters, and setting flags are often ignored or implied; with pseudocode, they are explicitly coded. The analyst using pseudocode would not, however, be concerned with language-dependent details such as the distinction between subscripts and indexes in COBOL, or the difference between real and integer numbers in FORTRAN. The idea is to describe the executable code in a form that a programmer can easily translate.

There is no standard pseudocode; many different versions exist. Most, however, incorporate the three structured programming conventions: sequence, decision, and repetition. We will use a hybrid pseudocode in this text, borrowing from COBOL, FORTRAN, and Pascal.

SEQUENCE

Perhaps the easiest way to define sequential logic is by coding a FORTRAN-like expression, for example:

$$COUNT = 0$$

or:

$$STOCK = STOCK + QUANTITY$$

Such details as the sequence of operations and the rules for using parentheses are also borrowed from FORTRAN; data names should be taken from the data dictionary and/or the list of inputs and outputs on the IPO diagram. If you feel more comfortable with another language, the conventions of that language would serve just as well.

Input and output instructions are explicitly defined in pseudocode. We will use:

READ data FROM source

and

WRITE data TO destination

where "data" is a list of variables, a data structure, or a record, and "source" and "destination" refer to a file or a data base.

88

Blocks of Logic

It is possible to write a number of pseudocode instructions and treat them as a single block; for example:

    COUNT = 0

    ACCUMULATOR = 0

might be assigned the block name INITIALIZE. Once this has been done, we can refer to the entire block as a single sequence instruction:

    PERFORM INITIALIZE

A block can contain any set of sequence, decision, and/or repetition logic. The general form of a PERFORM is:

    PERFORM block

To distinguish between formal subroutines and internal procedures, some analysts use:

    PERFORM block USING list

for a subroutine; "list" designates a list of variables passed between the calling routine and the subroutine.

To simplify our discussion of decision and repetition logic, we will refer to blocks of instructions rather than to the individual commands. Remember that a pseudocode block consists of one or more pseudocode instructions.

DECISION

The general format of a decision pseudocode block is:

    IF condition
        THEN
                PERFORM block-1
        ELSE
                PERFORM block-2
    ENDIF

For example:

```
IF HOURS > 40
    THEN
            PERFORM OVERTIME
    ELSE
            PERFORM REGULAR
ENDIF
```

A standard IF-THEN-ELSE structure is used, with the THEN block executed if the condition is true, and the ELSE block executed if the condition is false. Note the ENDIF. A feature of most pseudocodes is that each block of logic is clearly delimited. A decision block always begins with IF and ends with ENDIF; there is no ambiguity. Note also the use of indentation; it makes the block easy to read.

A pseudocode block can contain any combination of code, including a decision block. Thus it is possible to nest decision logic; for example:

```
IF condition-1
    THEN
            IF condition-2
                THEN
                        PERFORM block-a
                ELSE
                        PERFORM block-b
            ENDIF
    ELSE
            PERFORM block-c
ENDIF
```

Note how indentation highlights the relationship among these instructions. Note also how IF and ENDIF clearly delimit both decision blocks.

REPETITION

In structured English, we did not distinguish between the various forms of repetitive logic; in pseudocode, we do. The basic idea of repetitive code is that a block is executed again and again until a terminal condition occurs. DO WHILE logic tests for this terminal condition at the top of the loop; for example:

```
WHILE condition DO
    PERFORM block
ENDWHILE
```

Note the use of indentation and the way WHILE and ENDWHILE delimit the block. As an alternative, the REPEAT until structure tests for the terminal condition at the bottom of the loop:

```
REPEAT
    PERFORM block
UNTIL condition
```

Some analysts use a pseudocode structure much like a FORTRAN DO loop to define a count-controlled loop:

```
DO index = initial TO limit
    PERFORM block
ENDDO
```

Again, note the indentation and the ENDDO.

THE CASE STRUCTURE

A common programming problem involves selecting from among several alternative paths. For example, a program might be designed to process four different types of inventory transactions; imagine a control module that accepts a transaction and, based on a code, passes control to one of four lower-level routines. Although nested decision statements could be used to define this logic, IF-THEN-ELSE blocks tend to be difficult to follow when nesting goes beyond three or four levels. The case structure is a better option; its general form is:

```
SELECT variable
    CASE (value-1) block-1
    CASE (value-2) block-2
        .
        .
        .
    DEFAULT CASE block-n
ENDSELECT
```

The decision made by a case structure depends on the value of the variable specified by the word SELECT. If it contains "value-1", then block-1 is executed; if it contains "value-2", then block-2 is executed, and so on. The DEFAULT CASE is coded in the event that the variable contains none of the listed values. A case structure is delimited by ENDSELECT. Once again, indentation makes the structure easy to read. For example, the control module for the inventory program described above might be coded as:

91

```
SELECT TRANSACTION TYPE
    CASE (increase)  PERFORM  INCREASE  STOCK
    CASE (decrease)  PERFORM  DECREASE  STOCK
    CASE (add)       PERFORM  ADD RECORD
    CASE (delete)    PERFORM  DELETE RECORD
    DEFAULT CASE     PERFORM  TRANSACTION ERROR
ENDSELECT
```

A NOTE OF CAUTION

Pseudocode is very much like real code; thus programmers find it easy to use and to understand. This fact does, occasionally, lead to a problem, however. Many systems analysts were once programmers. These former programmers feel comfortable with pseudocode; in fact, they may feel too comfortable with pseudocode. Rather than using this tool as an aid for planning or designing a program, they write the code. As a result, the program is written twice: once in pseudocode and once in real code. Aside from being an obvious waste of time, double coding misses the point of program design; if the analyst worries about coding details, crucial design considerations may well be overlooked. Also, programmers tend to resent such overspecification—they want to be told what to code, and not how to code it.

Even if the pseudocode is well done, the programmers sometimes resent it. Specifying algorithms in what is essentially a high-level programming language does limit the programmer's flexibility. Often, the programmer will fail to distinguish between the analyst's coding technique and the analyst's design; the result may be criticism (even rejection) of a perfectly good design based on inappropriate criteria. If your programmers dislike pseudocode, consider using structured English or some other technique instead.

Pseudocode is an excellent tool for defining computational algorithms. It is not a good tool for describing control structures, particularly when several nested decisions are involved. In this text, we will use structured English or pseudocode primarily for the low-level, computational modules of a hierarchy chart.

REFERENCES

1. Gane, Chris and Sarson (1979). *Structured Systems Analysis: Tools and Techniques.* Englewood Cliffs, New Jersey: Prentice-Hall, Inc.

2. Gillett, Will D. and Pollack (1982). *An Introduction to Engineered Software.* New York: Holt, Rinehart and Winston.

3. Peters, Lawrence J. (1981). *Software Design: Methods and Techniques.* New York: Yourdon Press.

Module J

Program
Logic Flowcharts

FLOWCHARTING

A flowchart is a graphical representation of program logic. Four standard symbols are used (Fig. J.1); they are linked by flowlines that show the sequence and direction of flow. By convention, logic flows from the top down, and from left to right; arrowheads are added to the flowlines to indicate deviations from this standard pattern. Since arrowheads make a flowchart easier to read we will always use them, even when the conventions are followed.

Fig. J.1: *Basic flowcharting symbols.*

Symbol	Meaning	Explanation
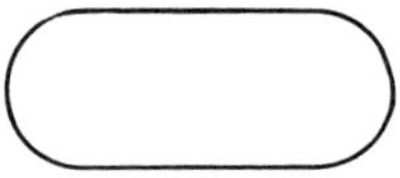	Terminal point	Marks the beginning or end of a program or program segment.
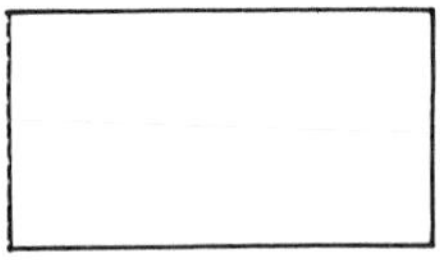	Process	Indicates any arithmetic or data copy operation.
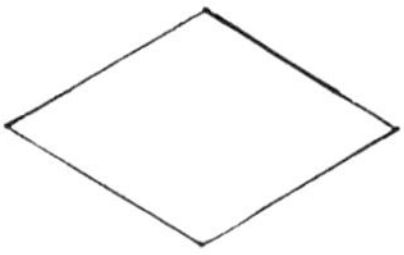	Decision	Indicates a yes/no decision to be made by the program.
	Input/output	Indicates any input or output operation.

Fig. J.2: *Sequence logic.*

Program logic can be expressed as combinations of three basic patterns: sequence, decision, and repetition. The sequence pattern (Fig. J.2) implies that the logic is executed in simple sequence, one block after another. A sequence block on a flowchart is identified by a rectangle, and can represent one or more actual instructions.

A decision block implies IF-THEN-ELSE logic (Fig. J.3). A condition (the diamond symbol) is tested. If the condition is true, the logic associated with the THEN branch is executed, and the ELSE block is skipped. If the condition is false the ELSE logic is executed and the THEN logic is skipped.

Fig. J.3: *Decision or*

IF-THEN-ELSE logic.

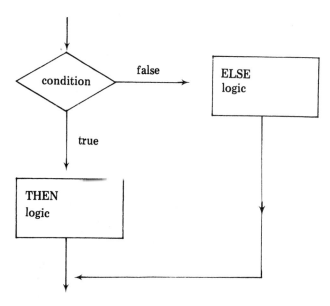

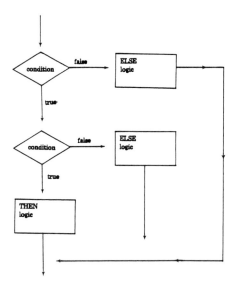

Fig. J.4: *Nested decision logic.*

Each decision block contains two sequence blocks: one for the THEN logic and one for the ELSE logic. A sequence block can contain one or more actual instructions. These instructions need not be limited to simple sequential logic; for example, on a high-level flowchart, a sequence block might be used to represent a subroutine containing sequence, decision, and repetitive logic. Taking advantage of this fact, we can expand the THEN branch of a decision block to contain another decision block (Fig. J.4): a nested IF. (Note that dashed lines have been added to Fig. J.4 to identify the position of the original THEN block.) Decision logic can be nested on the ELSE branch too (Fig. J.5), and nesting can occur on both paths.

Fig. J.5: *Another example of*

   nested decision logic.

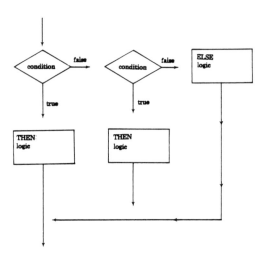

Fig. J.6: *DO WHILE logic.*

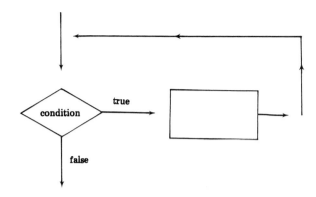

Fig. J.7: *DO UNTIL logic.*

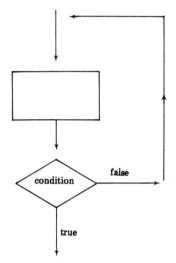

Two basic patterns exist for showing repetitive logic. In the DO WHILE pattern (Fig. J.6), a test is performed at the top of a loop. If the condition tested is true, then the logic of the loop is executed, and control is returned to the top for another test; if the condition is false, the logic of the loop is skipped, and control is transferred to the block following the DO WHILE. The DO UNTIL pattern (Fig. J.7) is different in that the test is performed at the bottom of the loop; otherwise the rules are similar.

A program is ultimately composed of combinations of these three basic structures. Program logic flows from block to block. Each block should have a single entry point (at the top) and a single exit; in other words, once the logical flow enters a block, it stays there until the function is completed. Simple sequence, decision, and repetition blocks can be combined to form larger blocks; for example, each module on a hierarchy chart can be viewed as a block of logic that performs a single, complete function. Even at this level, however, a block should have a single entry point and a single exit.

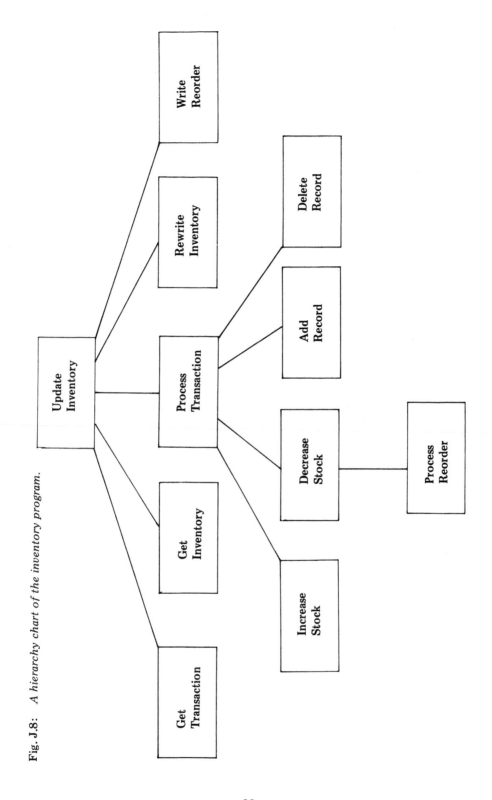

Fig. J.8: *A hierarchy chart of the inventory program.*

FLOWCHARTING: USES AND LIMITATIONS

A properly prepared flowchart can illustrate logical flow at a glance; in fact, many texts use simple flowcharts to clarify elements of structured English or pseudocode. In spite of this fact, flowcharting has fallen into disrepute. Why? The problem is a long history of misuse. For years, a detailed flowchart was standard documentation for a program, and programmers were required to prepare them. All too often, the flowchart was drawn after the program was written, and did little more than echo the code. A single flowchart tracing the complete logic of a program at a detailed level is too complex to follow, and impossible to maintain; such flowcharts are a waste of time and effort.

In this text, we will not attempt to develop a flowchart of the logic of a complete program. Instead, a hierarchy chart will be used to provide an overview of the program. Each block on the hierarchy chart represents one logical function, and an IPO chart is used to describe the details. For certain logical structures, a flowchart may well be the simplest, clearest way to define a process at the level of the IPO chart. Flowcharts are particularly good for decision-based algorithms, where the number of alternative paths does not exceed two or three. Flowcharts are a waste of time on algebraic algorithms, where no decisions are involved; algebraic expressions, structured English, or pseudo code are much better. (In other words, if you must write the algebraic expression anyway, why draw a box around it?) Complex case structures are better defined with a decision tree or a decision table. We will limit the use of flowcharts to relatively simple decision or control structures, usually at a high level in the hierarchy chart.

Incidently, most flowcharting standards mention two additional symbols: the connector and the off-page connector. We won't use them. If a flowchart is sufficiently complex to require connector symbols, it almost certainly describes too much logic for a single IPO chart. If the problem involves a series of arithmetic steps, then algebra, structured English, or pseudo code are better choices.

SOME EXAMPLES

In Module H, a hierarchy chart for an inventory program was developed; it is repro-duced as Fig. J.8. The main control module, Update Inventory, determines the order in which the second level modules are executed; Fig. J.9 shows a flowchart of the process. Note that the first four modules are always executed in simple sequence, but that the Write Reorder module is conditional; a flowchart allows the reader to de-termine at a glance the logic of such control structures.

The Process Transactions module (Fig. J.10) represents a somewhat more com-plex control structure; had more than four decisions been involved, we would not have used a flowchart. As we move down to Decrease Stock, we see that the flowchart (Fig. J.11) clearly shows an arithmetic operation followed by a decision. We would probably not use a flowchart for Increase Stock, however, since only the arithmetic operation is required.

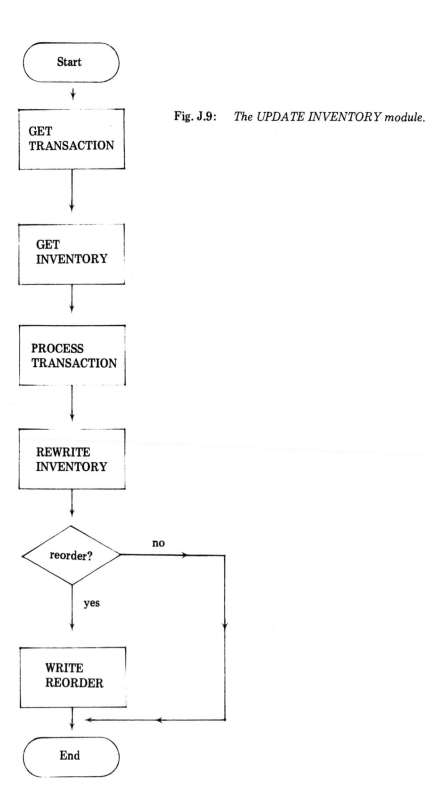

Fig. J.9: *The UPDATE INVENTORY module.*

100

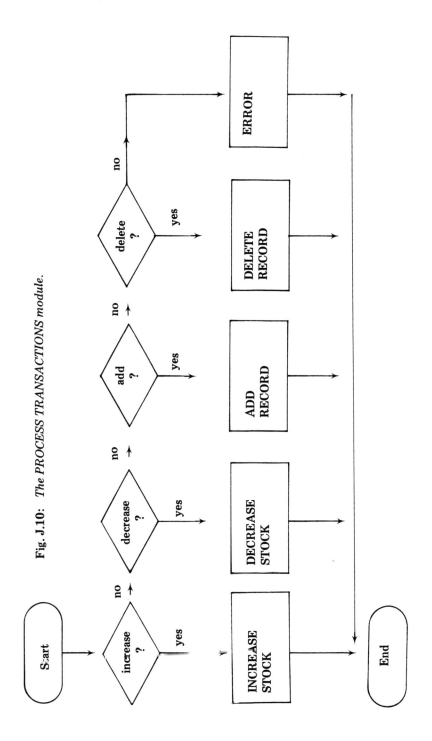

Fig. J.10: *The PROCESS TRANSACTIONS module.*

101

Fig. J.11: *The DECREASE STOCK module.*

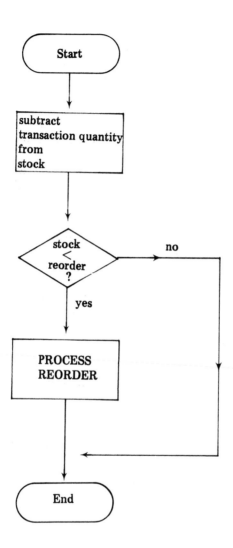

REFERENCES

1. Bohl, Marilyn (1978). *Tools for Structured Design.* Chicago: Science Research Associates, Inc.

Warnier/Orr Diagrams

WITH: *David C. Haddad*

OUTLINE

WARNIER-ORR DIAGRAMS

As an alternative to HIPO, many analysts prefer the Warnier-Orr design methodology. Developed in the early 1970s by Jean-Dominique Warnier and extended to system design by Ken Orr, this technique has enjoyed wide acceptance in France and, recently, in the United States. This introduction is merely an overview of the technique; additional details can be found in the references listed at the end of the module.

At first glance, a Warnier-Orr diagram seems like a hierarchy chart turned on its side. For example, Fig. K.1 shows a portion of a hierarchy chart for a simple program, while Fig. K.2 shows the equivalent Warnier-Orr diagram. Read the diagram from left to right. The program is divided into five high level modules: *Get Transaction*, *Get Master Record*, *Process Transaction*, *Write New Master*, and *Produce Report*. One of these modules, Get Transaction, is itself broken into a number of lower-level modules. The symbol { that groups these low-level modules with their parent is called a brace, though some would call it a bracket or a parenthesis. Note how the structure closely resembles the hierarchy chart.

A hierarchy chart describes only the program structure; it says nothing about the logical flow. A Warnier-Orr diagram does. Consider the sequence in which modules are invoked. Read the Warnier-Orr diagram (Fig. K.2) from top to bottom; *Get Transaction* is executed first, *Get Master Record* second, and so on. How often is each module executed? Note the numbers under the module names in Fig. K.2; they indicate the number of times the module is repeated on each program cycle. For example, each time the program is repeated, *Get Transaction* is executed once, and each time *Get Transaction* is invoked, *Read Transaction* is executed once.

A Warnier-Orr diagram can be used to describe a data structure, a set of detailed program logic, or a complete program structure; it is a flexible tool. Before we illustrate how Warnier-Orr diagrams can be used to help design a system or a program, we will begin with the basics, and discuss data structures and program logic; then we'll consider an example.

Defining Data Structures

A key principle in the Warnier-Orr methodology is that the design and structure of a well-written program are tied to the structure of the data; thus the designer typically begins with the data structures. For example, assume that an application calls for processing library circulation data. Each of a large number (N) of potential borrowers might have several books checked out. For each book, we must keep the call number, title, and author. Figure K.3 shows a Warnier-Orr diagram describing the hierarchical structure of these data. The numbers under the data element names show that data are maintained for N borrowers; that each borrower has K (a variable number of) books; and that for each book, one call number, one title, and one author are kept. A similar structure can be developed for most data.

Defining Program Logic

At a detailed level, a program consists of logic instructions. Any programming task can be defined by combinations of three elementary constructs: sequence, decision, and

Fig. K.1: *A typical hierarchy chart.*

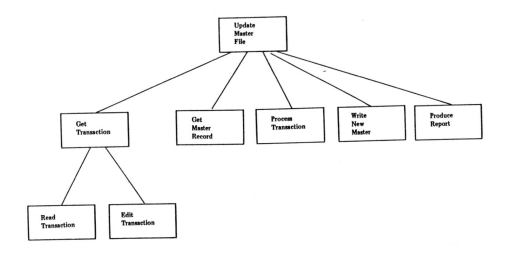

Fig. K.2: *An equivalent Warnier-Orr Diagram.*

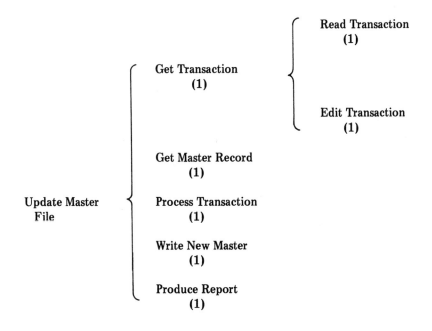

repetition. Let's consider how Warnier-Orr diagrams can be used to show each of these basic program logic blocks.

Figure K.4 shows both a flowchart and the equivalent Warnier-Orr diagram for a sequence operation. The (1) under READ A on the Warnier-Orr diagram indicates that this instruction is executed once.

The decision structure is illustrated in Fig. K.5; once again, a flowchart is included for comparison. Near the top of the diagram is the line:

$$A{>}0 \left\{ B{=}\sqrt{A} \right.$$

Under this line are the numbers (0,1), which tell us that the expression $B{=}\sqrt{A}$ is executed either 0 or 1 times, depending on whether the condition, $A{>}0$, is true or false. Near the bottom is another line:

$$\overline{A{>}0} \left\{ \text{WRITE ERROR} \right.$$

Fig. K.3: *The hierarchical structure of library circulation data.*

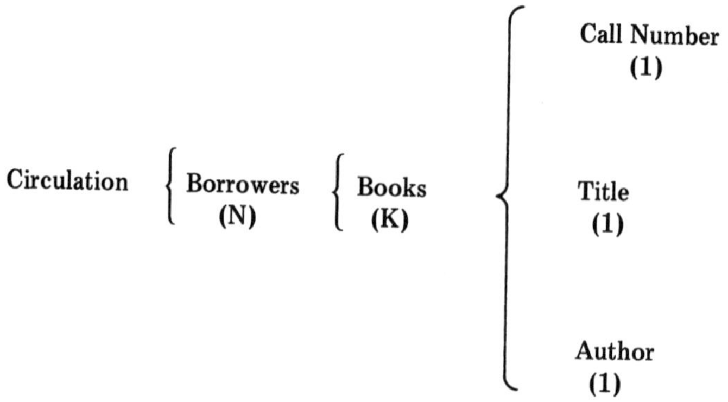

$$\text{Circulation} \left\{ \text{Borrowers} \atop (N) \right. \left\{ \text{Books} \atop (K) \right. \left\{ \begin{array}{l} \text{Call Number} \\ (1) \\ \\ \text{Title} \\ (1) \\ \\ \text{Author} \\ (1) \end{array} \right.$$

106

Fig. K.4:   *Sequence.*

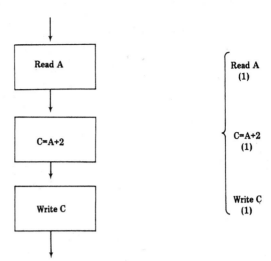

Fig. K.5:   *Decision.*

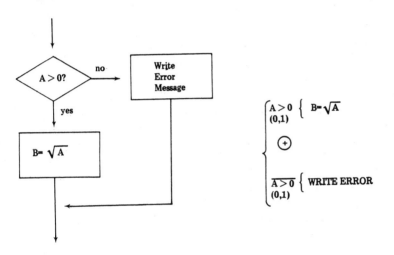

Fig. K.6:   *Repetition.*

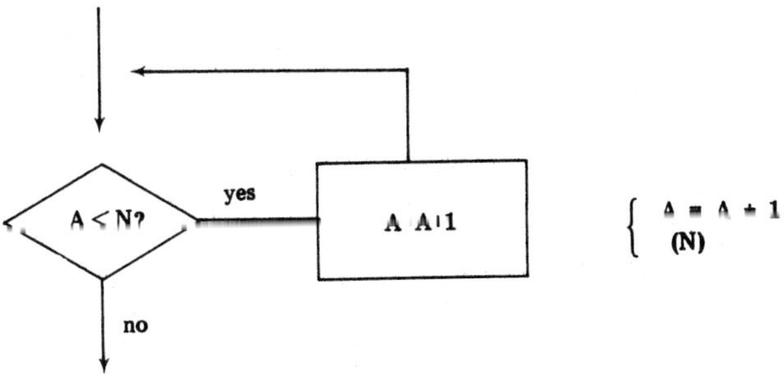

The horizontal line above the condition negates the condition; in other words, $\overline{A>0}$ means "A not greater than zero." Once again, the numbers (0,1) are found below the condition; the process WRITE ERROR is invoked 0 or 1 times depending, on whether the condition is true or false. Finally, note the "plus sign in a circle" ($\oplus$) between the two lines of the Warnier-Orr diagram (Fig. K.5). This is an *exclusive or* symbol. Either A is greater than 0, or it isn't; the two conditions are mutually exclusive. This is how IF-THEN-ELSE logic is represented on a Warnier-Orr diagram.

It is possible to indicate that multiple expressions follow a given condition, for example:

$$A>0 \begin{cases} B=\sqrt{A} \\ (1) \\ \\ B=B+1 \\ (1) \end{cases}$$

Note that a group of statements is enclosed by the brace or bracket that follows the condition.

Figure K.6 illustrates the repetition (DO WHILE) structure. The (N) below A=A+1 tells us that it is executed a variable number of times; if the program logic called for repeating a set of logic 10 times, we would have written (10) below the expression.

AN EXAMPLE

Now that certain basic ideas have been introduced, let's use an example to illustrate how the Warnier-Orr methodology might support the design process. In Module H, the HIPO documentation for an inventory program was developed; we'll use this same example again. Let's assume that the physical implementation chosen for the system calls for two programs, an on-line inventory update program and, an exception report generation program. Five major functions can be identified for the inventory update program, while the report generation program simply reads, formats, and writes the reorder records; these functions are summarized in the system-level Warnier-Orr diagram of Fig. K.7.

According to the Warnier-Orr methodology, the key to designing a program is the data structure. What major data flows are associated with the functions described in Fig. K.7? Basically, transaction and inventory data are read and processed, and reorder data are generated; these major data flows can be added to the diagram (Fig. K.8). If we can define the structure of each of these major data flows, we should be able to use the structures to design the programs.

Fig. K.7: *The high-level structure of the inventory system.*

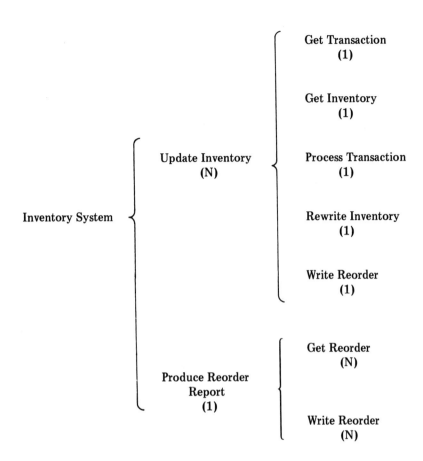

Defining the Data Structure

It is best to start with the output data. Why? Because the objective of the program (or the system) is to produce that output. Any data elements in the output must enter the system through one of the inputs. Thus, by beginning with the output, we define the minimum data the system must contain. The ultimate output from the system is an inventory exception report. What data elements does this report contain? (Note: check the data dictionary.) As a minimum, we can identify the part number, part description, reorder quantity, price, primary supplier, and secondary supplier; the structure of this report is summarized in Fig. K.9.

What is the source of the exception report? The *Produce Reorder Report* program. Where does this program get its data? Figure K.8 shows the input to this program is *Reorder*, so *Reorder* must contain all the data elements found in *Exception Report*. Note that there is one exception report (or one reorder file) containing an unknown

109

Fig. K.8: *The high-level structure of the inventory system with major inputs, outputs, and data flows.*

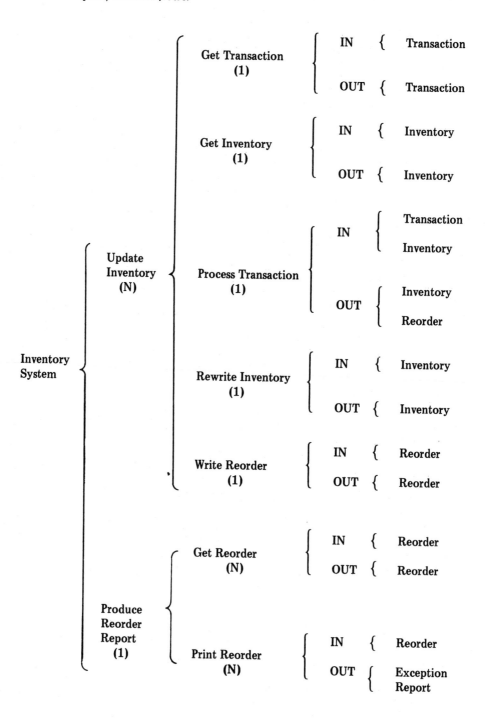

The structure of the Exception Report. Note that the Reorder Data flow has the same structure.

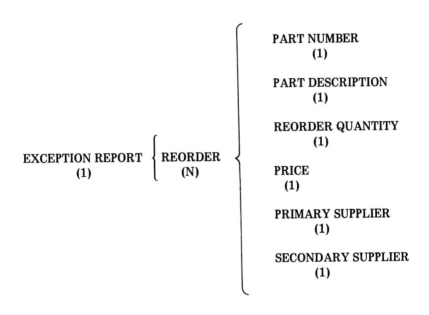

number of reorder records, and that each reorder record contains one part number, one part description, and so on.

What is the source of the reorder flow? Keep reading up the rightmost column of the inventory system diagram until you find a module that produces *Reorder* as its output. We can ignore *Write Reorder*, as its only input is *Reorder*. Look at *Process Transaction*, however. The inputs are *Transaction* and *Inventory*; clearly these two data flows must supply the data elements of *Reorder*. The structure of an inventory record is shown in Fig. K.10; note that the first six data elements match Reorder. Additionally, the system needs the stock on hand and the reorder point, and *Inventory* seems the only reasonable place to put them.

The structure of a transaction is a bit more complex. The system must process four different types of transactions: an increase to stock, a decrease from stock, an addition of a new part, or a deletion of an existing part. The data elements contained in a transaction vary with the transaction type (Fig. K.11). Note that there is one transaction file containing Q transactions. A transaction can be any one of four types; the (0,1) below each transaction type indicates that the substructure can occur either 0 or 1 times, and the exclusive or symbols imply that for any given transaction, one and only one of these structures can exist.

Fig. K.10: *The structure of an INVENTORY record.*

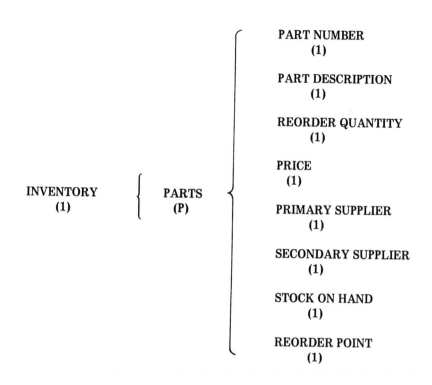

The Report Generation Program

Now that the data structures have been defined, we can begin to design the programs. We'll start with the report generation program. Ideally, the design of a program should be based on the structure of its input data. The only input to the report generation program is *Reorder*, which has the same structure as the output exception report (Fig. K.9). There is one reorder file containing N reorders; that suggests a repetitive data structure. Move over to the decomposition of *Reorder*, and note that all the data elements occur only once. The data structure suggests a very simple program that repeats until there are no more reorders; we are looking at a read, format, and write loop.

The program itself is described in Fig. K.12. It is divided into three primary functions—begin, process, and end. The processing loop repeats N times, once for each reorder. Read the Warnier-Orr diagram from left to right and from top to bottom; you should have little trouble relating the structure to a simple report generation program. As an exercise, write the pseudocode or structured English for this program.

Fig. K.11:   *The Transaction structure.*

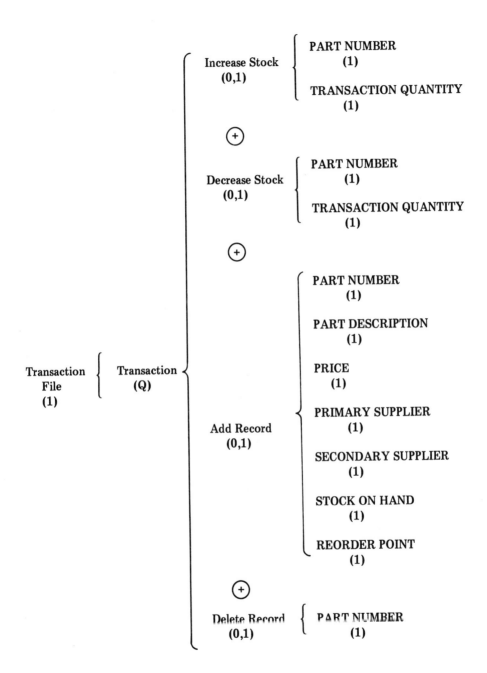

Fig. K.12: *The Produce Reorder Report program.*

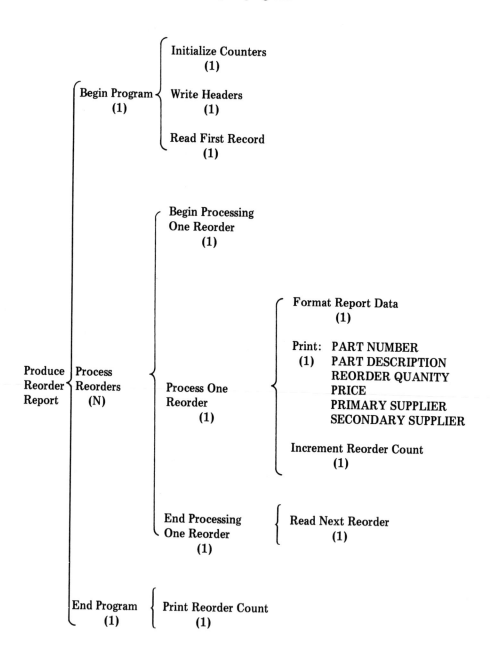

Incidently, if there is a difference in the structures of the input and the output data, which structure should be used as a model for the program? Normally, the input data structure is used. Why? Outputs are frequently subject to change. If the output data structure is used as a model for the program, a minor change in the data could require a major program modification. Generally, the input data are more stable.

The Inventory Update Program

Next we turn to the inventory update program. This on-line program will read a transaction, update the inventory master record associated with that transaction, and, where appropriate, identify and write reorder records. The primary input is a transaction (Fig. K.11). Look at the structure of this data flow. At the highest level, the number of transactions is unknown, suggesting that the main control module will contain repetitive logic and loop until there are no more transactions. The next level involves a decision, with a link to one of four lower-level modules, depending on the transaction type. (Note: a typical on-line program resides in main memory. A polling signal alerts the program when a transaction is ready to be processed; you might view the logic as a continuous loop, with the program sitting in core and waiting for input.)

Are there any other inputs to the inventory update program? Yes, *Inventory*. Look at the structure of an inventory record (Fig. K.10). Except for the lack of a decision block, it resembles the *Transaction* structure; there is no apparent incompatibility in the two data flows. The output is *Reorder*, and its structure also resembles *Transaction*. Thus we can safely use the structure of *Transaction* as a model in designing the program (Fig. K.13).

Let's follow the Warnier-Orr diagram as a single transaction is processed. (Remember to read the diagram from top to bottom and from left to right.) We'll assume that any necessary initialization functions have been done; thus we begin near the middle of the second column from the left (Fig. K.13) with *Transaction*. What steps are involved in processing a transaction? Move one column to the right. We begin processing by getting the transaction. Next, assuming that the transaction does not add a new record to the inventory file (note the decision logic), we read an inventory record. We then process the transaction; let's assume it's a decrease in stock. The decision logic (moving to the right) determines the transaction type; a decrease stock transaction means that we subtract the transaction quantity from the stock on hand and then check to see if the stock has fallen below the reorder point. Based on this test, the reorder flag is set to either 0 or 1. Once the transaction has been processed, the next major step (note that we are back to column three) is to rewrite the inventory record. Finally, if the reorder flag is set to 1, we write a reorder record. This ends the processing of one transaction.

Obviously, many details have been ignored in developing the sample Warnier-Orr diagram; for example, we did not include a transaction type to modify any of the fields (other than STOCK ON HAND) of an existing master record. This was, after all, an introductory-level example, and we did not want to bury the concept in unnecessary details. How much detail should be included? It is a good idea to remember the purpose of a Warnier-Orr diagram: to design and develop the structure of the system or the program. The intent is not to include every programming detail. We want to map the system, not implement it. Given enough practice, you will develop your own style

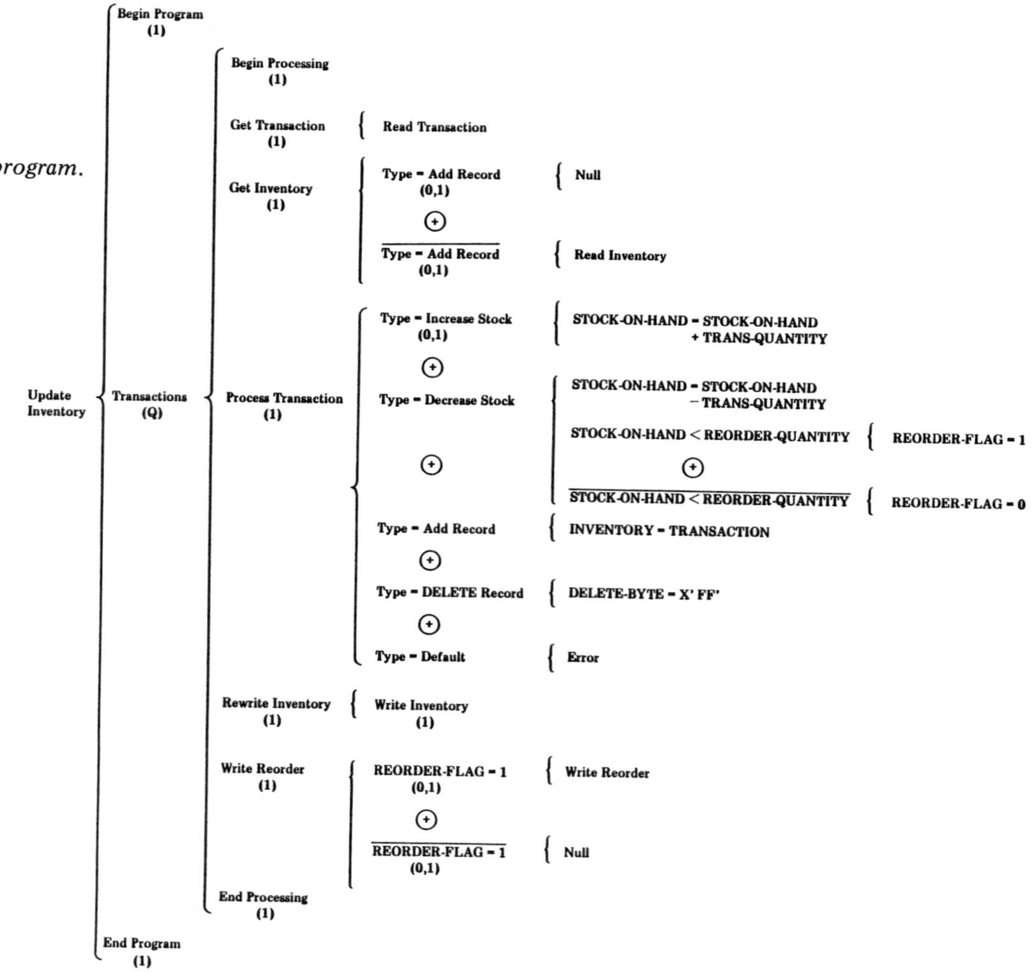

Fig. K.13: *The UPDATE INVENTORY program.*

Update Inventory {

- Begin Program (1)
- Transactions (Q) {
  - Begin Processing (1)
  - Get Transaction (1) { Read Transaction
  - Get Inventory (1) {
    - Type = Add Record (0,1) { Null
    - ⊕
    - ¬(Type = Add Record) (0,1) { Read Inventory
  - Process Transaction (1) {
    - Type = Increase Stock (0,1) { STOCK-ON-HAND = STOCK-ON-HAND + TRANS-QUANTITY
    - ⊕
    - Type = Decrease Stock {
      - STOCK-ON-HAND = STOCK-ON-HAND − TRANS-QUANTITY
      - ⊕ {
        - STOCK-ON-HAND < REORDER-QUANTITY { REORDER-FLAG = 1
        - ⊕
        - ¬(STOCK-ON-HAND < REORDER-QUANTITY) { REORDER-FLAG = 0
    - Type = Add Record { INVENTORY = TRANSACTION
    - ⊕
    - Type = DELETE Record { DELETE-BYTE = X' FF'
    - ⊕
    - Type = Default { Error
  - Rewrite Inventory (1) { Write Inventory (1)
  - Write Reorder (1) {
    - REORDER-FLAG = 1 (0,1) { Write Reorder
    - ⊕
    - ¬(REORDER-FLAG = 1) (0,1) { Null
  - End Processing (1)
- End Program (1)

}

and learn to include enough detail to support writing the pseudocode or structured English, but not so much as to obscure the design.

Expect to complete several drafts of your Warnier-Orr diagram before an acceptable design emerges; no one, not even the most experienced systems analyst, can design a system in one shot. Start with rough sketches on a chalkboard or with paper and pencil; you will be more likely to throw away your false starts and begin again if your initial diagrams are rough. Only when the system begins to make sense should you attempt to develop neat Warnier-Orr diagrams.

STRUCTURE CLASH

In our sample program, the structures of the input and output data were similar, and thus the design of the program was straightforward. Often, with more complex programs, the structures of the input and output data differ radically; this is called a *structure clash*. When the structures clash, it is difficult to design a program. A common solution is to create an intermediate data store or data file with a structure that does not clash with either the input or the output. The program can then be split in two, with the input processed to intermediate form, and the intermediate data subsequently processed into the desired output.

SCIENTIFIC PROGRAMMING

A common problem in scientific programming is that neither the input nor the output data have a structure; the input is often an array of numbers, and the output a single value or a set of statistics. The key to such programs is usually a mathematical model or algorithm. The design of such programs should be based on the structure of the algorithm rather than the structure of the data; Warnier-Orr diagrams can still prove useful, however.

REFERENCES

1. Higgins, David A. (1979). *Program Design and Construction.* Englewood Cliffs, New Jersey: Prentice-Hall, Inc.

2. Orr, Kenneth T. (1981). *Structured Requirements Definition.* Topeka, Kansas: Ken Orr and Associates, Inc.

3. Orr, Kenneth T. (1977). *Structured Systems Development.* New York: Yourdon, Inc.

4. Warnier, Jean-Dominique (1976). *The Logical Construction of Programs.* New York: Van Nostrand Reinhold.

5. Warnier, Jean-Dominique (1978). *Program Modification.* London: Martinus Nijhoff.

Module L

PERT and CPM

WITH: *Teruo Fujii*

OUTLINE

PROJECT MANAGEMENT

Managing a complex project can be very difficult. Often, the best approach is to break it into a series of small tasks that are more easily controlled or managed. The danger with such subdivision is that it becomes too easy to focus on the individual tasks or activities, thus losing sight of the whole project. A tool is needed to support the subdivision into smaller tasks or activities, while preserving an overall view. PERT and CPM are two of the better known techniques.

PERT (Program Evaluation and Review Technique) gained prominence during the late 1950s when it proved invaluable in scheduling and controlling the highly complex Polaris missile project. It is particularly useful in research and development projects where the times required to complete the various activities are uncertain. CPM (Critical Path Method), on the other hand, is most useful in situations where the duration of the project can be controlled by increasing or decreasing resources; for example, by pouring more money into a car, it might be possible to finish a 500-mile race in a shorter time. Basically, PERT should be used when the activity times are highly uncertain, and CPM when prior history or experience makes the activity times relatively well-defined.

The key to both PERT and CPM is the project network. The basic idea is to break the project into logical steps or activities, and then to order these activities into a sequence. The project network is a graphic tool for describing this sequence.

AN EXAMPLE

Perhaps the easiest way to gain an understanding of how to develop and use a project network is through an example. Imagine that you have been assigned the task of painting an old-fashioned, rectangular, wooden army barracks. You'll have fifteen soldiers under your command. The job involves three distinct steps. First, the old, loose paint must be scraped from the walls. Next, the new paint is applied. Finally, razor blades are used to remove excess paint from the window panes. The problem is compounded by limited materials; you'll have only five scrapers, five paint brushes, and five razor blades.

One way to accomplish the task might be to scrape all the walls first, then paint all the walls, and finally remove the excess paint from all the windows. This would be very inefficient, however. We have fifteen soldiers, and only five of any one tool; thus, if we do one task at a time, ten soldiers will always be idle. Another, less obvious problem arises from the fact that the best time to remove paint from a window pane is shortly after it has been applied; after the paint has hardened, removing it becomes much more difficult. There must be a better way.

Why not work on one side at a time? The first logical activity is scraping the loose paint; thus we'll have five soldiers pick up the scrapers while the other ten relax. As soon as the first side has been scraped, the first five soldiers can move on to side two, while a second contingent picks up the paint brushes and begins to apply the paint. Now, only five soldiers are resting. Later, as the scrapers move to side three and the painters to side two, the last five soldiers can begin to remove the excess paint with the razor blades. With everyone working, the job should be finished in less time.

120

The barracks is rectangular, with the long sides twice as long as the short. Also, the jobs are not equivalent; painting takes longer than scraping, which takes longer than razoring. Let's assume that we have estimated the activity times shown in Fig. L.1, and develop a simple *Gantt chart* or *bar chart* (Fig. L.2) to illustrate a plan for completing the work. Note that scraping begins at time zero, and ends twelve hours later. Painting begins at the end of the second hour, after the first side has been scraped, and ends eighteen hours later at the end of hour twenty. Razoring is dependent upon painting; it makes little sense to remove paint from windows until after the paint has been applied. Note the intermittent activity of the razor wielders as indicated on the Gantt chart. The relationship between painting and razoring is not explicit, but implied.

Read the Gantt chart. A horizontal line following an activity shows when a given group of soldiers is active; the absence of a line denotes a rest period. The total elapsed time for the project is twenty-two hours. How long would it take without planning? Scraping would take twelve hours, painting eighteen, and cleaning six more, for a total time of thirty-six hours. Planning and coordination yield definite benefits.

Fig. L.1: *Time estimates (in hours) for painting a barracks.*

	Scraping	Painting	Razoring
Sides 1 and 3	2	3	1
Sides 2 and 4	4	6	2

Fig. L.2: *A Gantt chart or bar chart for the barracks painting project.*

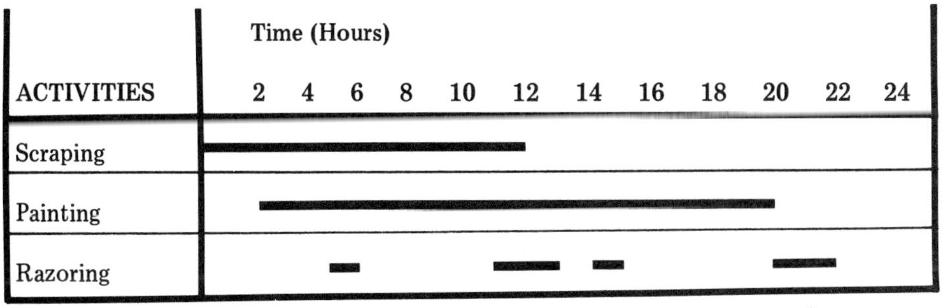

ACTIVITIES	Time (Hours) 2 4 6 8 10 12 14 16 18 20 22 24
Scraping	
Painting	
Razoring	

The Project Network

The *project network* (Fig. L.3) extends the capabilities of the bar chart. Like the bar chart, it depicts activities, and their starting and completion times. However, the project network explicitly illustrates how activities depend on each other, whereas the bar chart simply implies this activity dependence; this is what makes the project network so much more powerful as a tool for systems analysis and design.

A project network is quite easy to follow. The activities (painting, scraping, and razoring) are represented by lines or arrows, while *events* (the beginning or end of an activity) are represented by circles. For example, consider scraping the first side (Fig. L.3). It begins with event 1, and ends with event 2. The activity itself is identified by the numbers of its beginning and ending events; thus scraping the first side is activity 1-2. An event has no time duration and requires no resources; it is merely a definable instant in time. Activities, on the other hand, consume both time and resources.

Fig. L.3: *A project network for the barracks painting project.*

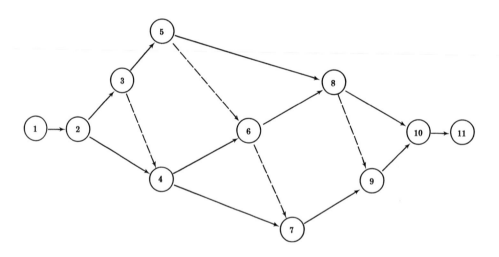

				Dummy activities
1-2	scrape side 1	5-8	scrape side 4	3-4
2-3	scrape side 2	6-8	paint side 3	5-6
2-4	paint side 1	7-9	razor side 2	6-7
3-5	scrape side 3	8-10	paint side 4	8-9
4-6	paint side 2	9-10	razor side 3	
4-7	razor side 1	10-11	razor side 4	

Follow the project network of Fig. L.3. Begin at the left. Activity 1-2 represents scraping the first side. When this activity is completed, two other activities can begin: 2-3 represents scraping the second side, and 2-4 represents painting the first side. Note that event 2 marks the end of activity 1-2 *and* the beginning of activities 2-3 and 2-4.

Focus on event 4, and note the dashed line linking events 3 and 4. Event 3 marks the end of scraping side two. Event 4 marks the end of painting the first side. Event 4 also marks the beginning of activity 4-6, paint side two. Before painting can begin on side two, both scraping side two (event 3) and painting side one (event 4) must be completed; there is a dependency relationship between events 3 and 4. Activity 3-4 shows this relationship, but consumes no time and no resources. It is a *dummy activity*.

Read through the rest of Fig. L.3, using the activity descriptions printed below the graphics as a key. Try to explain the reason for each of the dummy activities.

Dummies can also be used to link parallel activities in a network. Consider, for example, Fig. L.4, which shows a simple project network for starting an automobile. Activity 5-6 represents fastening seat belts. When must the belts be fastened? On most cars, at any time. Near the top of Fig. L.4 is a project network that shows event 5 "hanging out there," with no apparent relationship to the best of the network. Below it is another version with a dummy activity, 2-5, added. It makes the network a bit easier to read.

Fig. L.4: *Dummy activities can be used to link parallel activities to the project net-*

work.

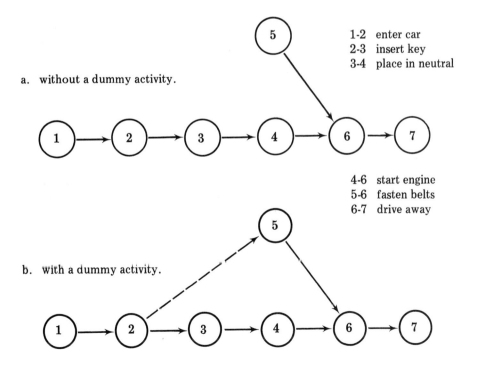

a. without a dummy activity.

1-2   enter car
2-3   insert key
3-4   place in neutral

4-6   start engine
5-6   fasten belts
6-7   drive away

b. with a dummy activity.

123

Estimating Activity Times

The project network shows the relationships between the various activities and events. At a glance, it is possible to see how a given event depends upon the completion of one or more activities. The next step is to estimate the activity times.

In most practical situations, an experienced systems analyst can make a reasonably accurate estimate of the probable duration of each activity. By laying out the project network, the analyst is breaking the project into a series of relatively brief, discrete steps, and estimates made on such small elements are often quite accurate. It is possible, however, that an analyst may feel uncertain about an activity's likely duration. When this happens, the PERT technique suggests using three different estimates: optimistic, most likely, and pessimistic. (Perhaps several different experts might be asked to supply a best guess, and the extremes used along with the average.) Once the three estimates have been generated, they can be plugged into the following formula:

$$\text{Event time} = \left[\frac{\textit{Optimistic} + (4 * \textit{most likely}) + \textit{pessimistic}}{6} \right]$$

to calculate the event times to be used in the project network.

Let's add time estimates (Fig. L.1) to the project network for the barracks painting problem; the new project network is shown in Fig. L.5. Note that there is no relationship between the length of an arrow representing an activity and the time estimate associated with it. The arrows show dependency relationships, while the number above the arrow represents activity time.

Scheduling the Project

Once the project network is completed, the analyst can begin to use it as an aid to scheduling. The first step is to compute two statistics for each event: the *earliest event time (EET)* and the *latest event time (LET)*.

The earliest event time represents the earliest time an event can possibly begin; conventionally, it is zero for the first event. For all others, the EET is computed by using three simple rules:

1. Select all activities entering the event.

2. For each entering activity, sum the activity's duration and the EET of its initial event.

3. Select the highest EET obtained.

124

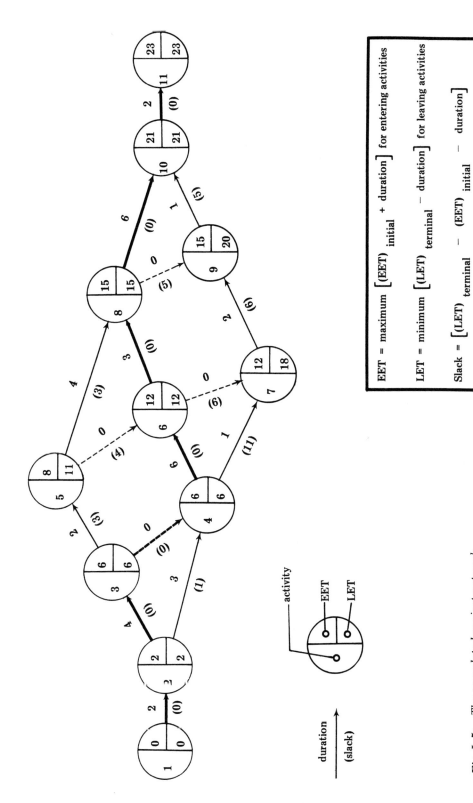

$$EET = \text{maximum} \begin{bmatrix} (EET)_{\text{initial}} + \text{duration} \end{bmatrix} \text{ for entering activities}$$

$$LET = \text{minimum} \begin{bmatrix} (LET)_{\text{terminal}} - \text{duration} \end{bmatrix} \text{ for leaving activities}$$

$$Slack = \begin{bmatrix} (LET)_{\text{terminal}} - (EET)_{\text{initial}} - \text{duration} \end{bmatrix}$$

Fig. L.5:   *The completed project network.*

125

For example, event 2 has only one entering activity, 1-2 (see Fig. L.5). Logically, what is the earliest time this event can begin? When activity 1-2 is completed. The earliest event time for event 1 is (by definition) zero. The duration of activity 1-2 is estimated at two hours. Activity 1-2 cannot begin before time zero, and will consume two hours; thus it cannot possibly end before time two. Event 2 marks the end of activity 1-2; thus the EET for event 2 must be two hours after the project begins.

Let's consider another example of the earliest event time calculation; we'll focus on event 7. There are two entering activities: 4-7 and 6-7. Prior calculations have shown that event 4 cannot begin before hour six; since activity 4-7 takes one hour, it cannot possibly be finished before hour seven. We also know that event 6 cannot begin before hour twelve, and that activity 6-7, a dummy, requires zero hours; thus it cannot possibly be finished before hour twelve. Event 7 represents the completion of activities 4-7 and 6-7. The former might be completed by hour seven, but the other can't be finished until twelve hours have passed. Event 7 represents the completion of *both*; thus its earliest event time must be twelve, the higher number.

The computed earliest event time for each activity has been added to the project network of Fig. L.5; look to the upper right of the event circles. Take the time to confirm each calculation.

The latest event time represents the latest time an event can possibly begin without affecting the schedule for the project. By convention, the LET of the last or terminal event is equal to its earliest event time; thus both the EET and LET are twenty-three for event 11 (Fig. L.5). For all other events, the latest event time is computed by using the following rules:

1. Consider all activities leaving an event.

2. Subtract each activity's duration from the LET of its terminal event.

3. Select the smallest LET obtained.

For example, consider event 10. It has one leaving activity, 10-11. The latest event time for event 11 is twenty-three hours; the duration of activity 10-11 is two hours; thus the LET for event 10 is twenty-one hours.

The computed latest event times are shown at the lower right of each event in Fig. L.5. Let's verify the calculations for event 8. There are two leaving activities: 8-9 and 8-10. Consider 8-9 first. The previously calculated LET for event 9 is twenty hours. The duration of activity 8-9, a dummy activity, is zero; thus the computed LET for event 8 is twenty hours. Now consider activity 8-10. The LET for event 10 is twenty-one hours; the duration of activity 8-10 is six hours; thus the computed LET for event 8 is fifteen hours. Which number is correct, twenty or fifteen? The third rule says to select the smaller figure; thus fifteen hours is correct. The student should verify the other latest event times on Fig. L.5. Remember to start at the right and work backwards.

126

The Critical Path

Note that on several of the events shown on Fig. L.5, the earliest and latest event times are equal. These events define the *critical path*, which is marked by a double line. Events along this line must begin on time, and activities that lie on the critical path must require no more than the estimated duration, or the project will not be completed on time. When PERT is used, the critical path becomes the primary focus of management control; monitoring the critical events or milestones provides an early warning if the estimates are inaccurate. When CPM is used, the critical path defines those activities into which additional resources should be poured, as only by shortening the critical path can the project completion time be improved.

Slack Time

Activities not on the critical path can—to a point—start late or exceed their estimated durations without affecting the project's estimated completion time; this property is called *slack* or *float*. The total slack time for an activity is computed by subtracting its duration and the earliest event time of its initial event from the latest event time of its terminal event:

$$\text{Total slack} = \left[(\text{LET})_{\text{terminal}} - (\text{EET})_{\text{initial}} - \text{duration}\right]$$

Using Fig. L.5 as a reference, the slack times shown in Fig. L.6 can be computed. Slack is also shown enclosed in parentheses beneath the activity arrows of Fig. L.5.

Fig. L.6: *Computed slack times for the barracks painting project network.*

Event		LET (terminal)	EET (initial)	Duration	Slack
2-4	Paint side 1	6	2	3	1
3-5	Scrape side 3	11	6	2	3
4-7	Razor side 1	18	6	1	11
5-6	Dummy	12	8	0	4
5-8	Scrape side 4	15	8	4	3
6-7	Dummy	18	12	0	6
7-9	Razor side 2	20	12	2	6
8-9	Dummy	20	15	0	5
9-10	Razor side 3	21	15	1	5

How can an analyst or a manager use slack? One possibility is in scheduling. For example, consider the three activities 4-7, 7-9, and 9-10. All have considerable slack, and all involve razoring. Is it possible that scraping and razoring could be done by the same five soldiers without affecting the project schedule? If so, the job would require ten rather than fifteen soldiers, a significant improvement. Slack is also useful in management control. For any given activity, the slack shows the maximum time the schedule can slip without affecting the project's expected total completion time.

PERT AND CPM

The project network is the foundation of both PERT and CPM, and the basic concepts of critical path and slack are common to both. PERT is used when the activity times are uncertain; the techique serves as an early warning system, alerting the analyst and management to the possible impact as the actual times for the various activities become known. Industry developed CPM to help solve scheduling problems when the activity times are known more precisely. The emphasis is on cost minimization: How can we best allocate limited resources to complete the project in a reasonable time and at minimum cost? The user of CPM would certainly consider cutting resources from fifteen to ten soldiers while maintaining the projected schedule. The PERT user, while interested in cost control, would be more concerned with the accuracy of the estimates for such early activities as 1-2, 2-3, and 3-4, and might postpone the release of the extra soldiers until the successful, on-time completion of event 4 demonstrated the accuracy of the estimated durations.

The project network is, however, the key to both techniques. The analyst can benefit from preparing a project network, even if neither PERT nor CPM is used to its full extent. For example, consider the simple Gantt chart prepared earlier in the chapter (Fig. L.2). It showed an estimated project completion time of twenty-two hours, while the project network of Fig. L.5 estimated twenty-three. Why the difference? Although it is not obvious on the Gantt chart, a study of the project network should reveal that it takes longer to scrape side two than it does to paint side one. See if you can find the relevant activities. The advantage of a project network over a Gantt chart is that the project network explicitly defines the relationships between events and activities, while the Gantt chart merely implies them. Simply, a project network is an easy to prepare, easy to read, highly accurate tool for scheduling and managing a project.

REFERENCES

1. Hartman, W., Matthes and Proeme (1968). *Management Information Systems Handbook.* New York: McGraw-Hill Book Company.

2. PERT Coordinating Group (1963). *PERT: Guide for Management Use.* Washington, D.C.: US Government Printing Office, publication number 0-6980452.

3. Wiest, Jerome D., and Levy (1969). *A Management Guide to PERT/CPM.* Englewood Cliffs, New Jersey: Prentice-Hall, Inc.

File Design and Space Estimates

SECONDARY STORAGE

In this module, we will consider problems associated with storing files on such secondary device as magnetic tape, cassette, magnetic drum, magnetic disk, and diskette. Tape and cassette are limited to the sequential storage of data, and are used primarily for backup on non-hobby computer systems. Drum is a high speed, low capacity medium used mainly for special purpose applications such as paging on a virtual memory system. For the average analyst, disk and diskette are the most commonly used secondary storage devices, and thus we will concentrate on them.

DEFINING THE DATA STRUCTURES

During system design, physical files were identified. As part of detailed design, the analyst must specify the contents of these files. The first step is laying out the data structure or structures. Each file represents one or more data stores on the data flow diagram, and each store, in turn, defines one or more data elements. Detailed descriptions of these elements can be found in the data dictionary. Given this information, the analyst can compile a list of data elements that compose a single logical record in the file. The file is built around the resulting structure.

For example, consider a year-to-date file from a payroll system. The data elements that must be stored for each employee are shown in Fig. M.1. The year-to-date statistics are seven digit numbers with a maximum value of 99,999.99; the comma and the decimal point are not stored, but implied. The total length of the structure is 71 characters. The year-to-date file will consist of a series of these logical records, one for each employee.

At this point, the analyst might code the data structures in the source language to be used by the programmers.

Fig. M.1: *The data structure of a year-to-date payroll logical record.*

Element name	Length	Format
Social security number	9	character
Name	20	character
Year-to-date gross pay	7	99999V99
Year-to-date federal tax	7	99999V99
Year-to-date state tax	7	99999V99
Year-to-date local tax	7	99999V99
Year-to-date FICA tax	7	99999V99
Year-to-date net pay	7	99999V99

SELECTING A LOGICAL ORGANIZATION

The analyst's next task is to select a set of rules for organizing the file. One possibility is to use a *sequential organization*. As a sequential file is created, records are added one after another in chain-like fashion. Later, when these data are processed, they are read in the same fixed sequence. Records can be stored in time order, or sorted and stored by some key. The basic idea is that a sequential file must be processed in a fixed order; the only way to access record number 500 is to first access records 1 through 499. Thus, the speed with which a given record can be accessed is a function of its physical location on the file.

The analyst can also select a *direct* or *random organization* for the data. When a direct access file is used, each logical record is assigned a key that corresponds in some way to the physical location of the data on disk. Given this key, it is possible to store or retrieve a record without regard for its position on the file; for example, record number 500 can be accessed just as quickly and just as easily as any other record.

A third alternative is an *indexed file*. As the data are stored, an index is created linking each record's logical key to its physical address on disk; the index is then stored independently. Later, when the data must be retrieved, the index is read into main memory and searched by the logical key, the physical address of the record is extracted from the index, and the record is read directly. Often, the index is maintained in logical key order; if so, by following the index, key by key, it is possible to process such files sequentially.

Not every element of a given data structure must be stored on the same file. For example, consider a student grade history record. It probably contains the student's identification number, name, department of major, and other general information. Following these basic elements will be the course code, description, credit hours, and grade for *each* course the student has taken. How many such entries will be found? The answer depends on the student. A first semester freshman may have none. A second semester senior may have fifty, or even more. One option is storing each student's grade history as a variable length record. An alternative is a series of linked records (Fig. M.2). Each student has a master record containing basic data. Buried in this record is a pointer to the first of the grade records. The first grade record points, in turn, to the second, which points to the third, and so on, until the end of the chain is reached. Splitting a data structure between two or more files should be considered whenever a repeating substructure (such as the student course records) is present, or when a record must be accessed by several different keys; for example, a school might want to access student data by student number, department of major, or local address.

The wave of the future is *data base management*. The task of creating a data base is beyond the scope of this book; the author strongly recommends that any future systems analyst take a good data base course. Assuming that the data base exists, the analyst's main task will be defining the data structures. many of the physical details associated with file design can be ignored in a data base environment. In most organizations, a data base administrator is responsible for creating, maintaining, and controlling access to the data base; once the basic structures have been defined, the analyst should consult with this individual.

Fig. M.2:   *Linked records.*

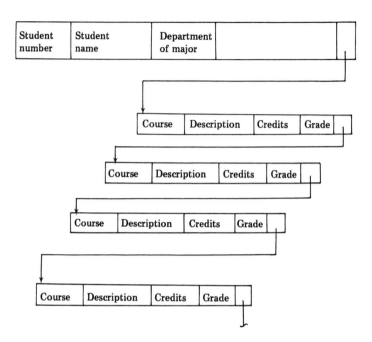

Selection Criteria

Which organization should the analyst select? The answer depends on the application, as each technique has its strengths and weaknesses. Generally, however, the analyst's objective should be to select the data organization that allows the system's functions to be performed at the lowest possible cost. In making this judgement, several factors, including physical storage costs, programming costs, execution costs, and usage costs, must be carefully evaluated and balanced; the concern must be with the *total cost*, not with any single element of that total.

Balancing cost factors is not always easy. For example, when disk is used, moving the read/write mechanism is a major component of execution cost. With well planned sequential files, head movement can be minimized, which suggests sequential access. Often, programmers feel more comfortable with sequential applications, meaning that programming costs will probably be lower than they might be if direct access were chosen. Even physical storage costs tend to favor sequential files, as the larger blocking factors possible on such files mean that the data will occupy less physical space. However, sequential files almost always require that data be processed in batch mode, and the delays inherent in waiting for the computer output can represent a significant user cost that far outweighs the apparent economies of a sequential file. Analysts have been grappling with the problem of balancing these cost factors for years, and have developed certain criteria that seem to suggest particular organizations.

Activity is a measure of the percentage of records in a file that are actually accessed each time the file is processed. It is a function of the required *turnaround* time. Some applications, such as payroll, can tolerate several days between collecting and processing data. Others, such as updating checking accounts, must be run at least daily. Still others require turnaround measured in hours, minutes, seconds, or even fractions of a second. The turnaround required by an application limits the amount of time during which transactions can be collected. If enough transactions occur during this interval, the file will be active; if not, it will be inactive. Highly active files should be organized sequentially; less active files call for a direct organization.

Turnaround is the time between the submission of a job and the return of the results. When this interval becomes very small, a few seconds or less, we stop thinking in terms of turnaround, and begin to concentrate on *response time*. If response time is an important factor in an application, it is likely that the system will be designed to process individual transactions in a random or unpredictable order. Sequential access simply will not do for such applications; direct or indexed access is essential.

Localized activity occurs when a significant percentage of a file's activity is concentrated in a relative handful of records. For example, an airline reservation file might contain data on numerous flights scheduled months in the future, but most customers will be interested in those few flights scheduled to leave within the next several days. When localized activity is expected, direct access is a good choice.

Another important factor is *flexibility*, which favors the indexed technique. When an indexed organization is used, records can be processed either sequentially or directly. Also, multiple indexes can be created; for example, student data might be indexed by student indentification number, department of major, and local address, and subsequently accessed by any of these keys. The indexed technique should not be used when a file is volatile, however. *Volatility* is a measure of the rate of additions to and deletions from the file; for example, a file listing current hit records would be quite volatile. On an indexed file, both the index and the data must be maintained; on sequential or direct files, only the data are involved.

File size is another concern. On disk, for example, direct access is achieved by moving an access arm over the track containing the desired record, and then reading the data as it rotates by. With a small file that occupies only a track or two, there is little advantage to be gained from direct access; it is almost as efficient to search the file sequentially. If sequential I/O instructions are easier for the programmers to code and debug, this factor may well offset the apparent advantages of direct access. In particular, consider using a sequential organization to hold table files. In contrast, consider how a massive, rarely used file might be stored. A sequential file on magnetic tape (or even microfiche) may well be the best answer.

Another important factor is the *status quo*. A new or unfamiliar file organization means that the programmers will have to be trained before they can use it. Additionally, implementing the system will probably take longer than if a more familiar organization were used. In selecting the new organization, the analyst should consider these extra costs. Similar arguments might be advanced for the existing hardware. The point is not to avoid change, but to recognize that change can be expensive.

Few files exist in a vacuum; most coexist with other, related files, and must be organized in a way that is compatible. Be careful to look beyond the single application, however. For example, consider payroll. The activity criterion might suggest a se-

133

quential organization, and in fact this might be the best choice for the transaction and year-to-date files. What about the personnel data, however? They are processed by the payroll application, but are needed by other systems as well. Perhaps the best choice is an indexed organization. The ultimate expression of concern for data *integration* is a data base.

These criteria are merely guidelines, not absolutes. They are the result of years of observation, trial, and error, and are in fact closer to folk wisdom than to science. Beginners often go overboard—the activity is high, and therefore the file must be organized sequentially. Don't forget that selecting a file organization is aimed at reducing the sum of several different costs, including the cost of storage, execution, programming, and usage. Selecting a file organization is perhaps the most important decision the analyst can make during detailed design. Take your time, and do it right.

PHYSICAL DATA STORAGE ON DISK

How are data physically stored on disk? That depends on the disk. Some systems divide the surface into a series of fixed length *sectors*. On many large computer systems a *fixed block architecture* is used; logically, there is little difference between the fixed block and sectored approaches, as both store data in fixed length units. Other disk units are *track addressed*. A track is one of the concentric circles around which data are stored on a disk surface. With a track addressed disk, space can be used in any way the programmer or analyst wishes. Track addressed disk is somewhat more flexible, allowing the programmer to fit the physical data structure to the requirements of the application. The sectored and fixed block approaches tend to be a bit easier to use.

When using a track addressed disk, the analyst can choose between a *count/data* or *count/key/data* format. Let's consider the count/data format first (Fig. M.3). For each record, two elements are stored: a count and the data. The count simply indicates the record's position relative to the beginning of the track; the first record is 00, the second is 01, and so on. A gap of unused space separates the count from the data. Imagine that a programmer wants record 04 on track 42. First, the access mechanism is moved to track 42. Next, the track is searched for count 04; when it is found, the

Fig. M.3: *The count/data format.*

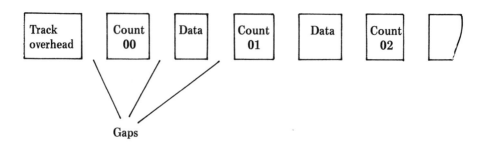

Gaps

data following it is transferred into the computer. The gap between the count and the data gives the disk's control unit enough time to read the count, check it, and then decide if the data should be accessed or ignored.

Sequential files are stored using the count/data format, as are direct access files that rely on relative record location; for example, COBOL's relative organization. If the programmer chooses to create and maintain an index listing the logical keys and their associated relative record numbers, an indexed file can be physically stored in count/data format, too.

The count/key/data structure (Fig. M.4) is an alternative. The count is still the relative position of the record on a track. The key is a logical entity that uniquely identifies the record, for example a social security number or a student identification number. The first step in accessing a record is still to move the read/write mechanism over the proper track. However, the track is then searched by key, rather than by count.

IBM's indexed sequential access method uses the count/key/data format. Many COBOL programmers are familiar with a direct data structure in which a relative track address and a logical key are provided to the system; this technique also uses count/key/data.

LOGICAL AND PHYSICAL DATA

A *physical record* is the unit of data transferred between main memory and an external device. A *logical record* is the unit of data needed by a single iteration of a program. Code is written to process logical records. Hardware moves physical records. While it is certainly possible that a logical record will be stored as a single physical record, it is not necessary. For example, on a track addressed disk, logical records can be blocked to form larger physical records (Fig. M.5). Why? Remember the gaps of unused space separating the physical records on the disk surface? Ten logical records stored without blocking call for ten sets of gaps. Ten logical records blocked and stored as a single

Fig. M.4:   *The count/key/data format.*

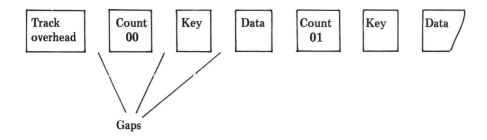

Gaps

135

Fig. M.5: *Blocking.*

10 records, unblocked:

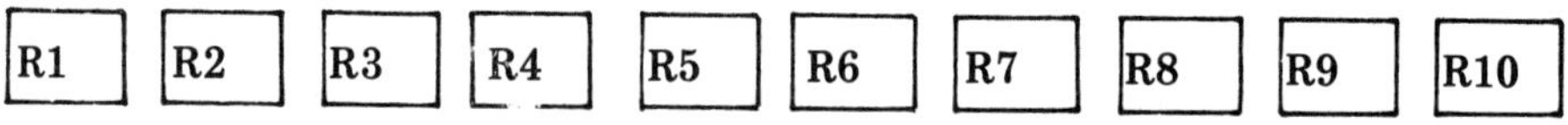

| R1 | R2 | R3 | R4 | R5 | R6 | R7 | R8 | R9 | R10 |

10 records blocked:

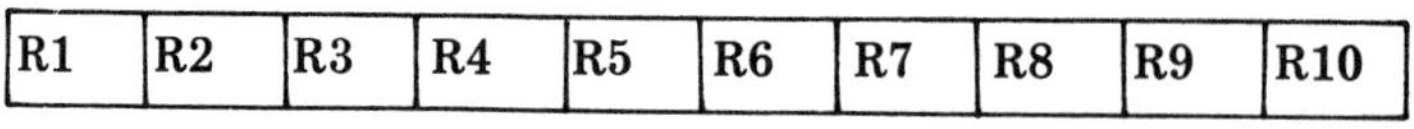

| R1 | R2 | R3 | R4 | R5 | R6 | R7 | R8 | R9 | R10 |

physical record require only one gap. With less wasted space, more data can be stored on a single track. Blocking several logical records to form a single physical record improves hardware efficiency.

On a sectored disk, a sector is the physical unit transferred between main memory and the external device. A common sector size on microcomputer systems is 256 characters or bytes. Storing one 71-character logical record in each sector would waste space. On many systems three such logical records are stored in each sector, thus utilizing 213 of the available 256 storage locations. What happens if a logical record is too big to fit in a sector? Often, a record can be *spanned* over two or more sectors. With blocking, reading a single *physical* record provides two or more *logical* records. With spanned records, accessing a single *logical* record involves reading two or more *physical* records.

The analyst must describe both the logical and the physical data. Programmers work with logical data, and program specifications must be developed during detailed design. It is the physical data that will actually be stored, however. Disk space is normally shared by many files; it is a scarce resource that must be carefully rationed. How much space should be assigned to a file? Is there enough space on a device to hold the necessary data? The analyst must answer these questions.

ESTIMATING SPACE REQUIREMENTS

Let's begin with a sectored disk or diskette. Earlier, the logical record length of a year-to-date record was determined to be 71 characters. If a sector can hold 256 characters, three complete records can be stored in each sector. How many records must be stored? In Chapter 2, employment at THE PRINT SHOP was estimated at 50 people. At three records per sector, how many sectors are needed to hold 50 records? Divide three into fifty: the answer is 16.67. Sixteen sectors are not enough; seventeen will be needed.

What is the capacity of a diskette? That depends on the system. Some small, single-sided 5.25 inch diskettes are designed to hold 160K characters per volume—that's about 640 sectors. Volumes with twice or even four times that capacity can be purchased. Hard disk drives, even for a microcomputer, are rated in megabytes; for example, a 1.6 megabyte disk would have 6400 sectors. The analyst should be familiar with the specifications of disk units used in his or her computer center.

In general, when a disk that stores sectors or fixed blocks is used, the amount of space needed to hold a file can be computed by the following rules:

1. Divide the sector size (or fixed block size) by the logical record length to get the number of records that will fit in a single sector. Ignore fractions, as only complete logical records are stored.

2. Divide the integer quotient from step 1 into the total number of logical records that must be stored in the file. Round the quotient up to the nearest whole number (for example, 15.25 becomes 16), since partial sectors cannot be assigned.

The result is the number of sectors needed by the file. The rules for estimating space on a fixed block architecture system are identical; the sector size is the only thing that changes.

What happens when large records must be spanned over two or more sectors? The rules change a bit, but the intent is still the same. Start by computing the number of sectors required for each logical record, and then multiply by the number of records in the file.

Estimating space requirements on a track addressed system is a bit more complex. In addition to the logical record length and the number of records in the file, yet another variable must be considered: the physical record length or block size. For example, let's use the 71 character logical record of Fig. M.1, and assume that 5000 such records must be stored. Initially, we'll assume that the data are not blocked; in other words, the physical record length is 71 characters.

The direct access device to be used in this example is an IBM 3330. The capacity of a track on an IBM 3330 is 13,030 characters or bytes. Using the count/data format, each record will consume a certain amount of overhead (for the count field and the gaps) plus the record length. The formula for computing the effective space required by each record is:

$$\text{space/record} = 135 + \text{data length}$$

With a data length of 71, each record will need the equivalent of 206 characters. Dividing 206 into the capacity of a track (13,030) yields a quotient of 63 plus a remainder; thus 63 records can be stored on each track. A total of 5000 records must be stored; how many tracks will be needed? Once again, divide; 5000 divided by 63 is

79 plus a fraction, meaning that more than 79 tracks will be needed, so 80 tracks should be assigned to the year-to-date file.

One point in these calculations might be a bit confusing. When computing the number of records per track, we truncated, essentially discarding the fractional part of the answer. Later, when computing the number of tracks, we rounded the answer up to the next larger integer. That seems inconsistent, but it isn't. The rule is that every physical record must be stored as a single entity. The only way we can use the fractional part of a track is by storing a piece of a record, and that is illegal. We compute the total number of tracks by dividing the number of records in the file by the number of *complete* records that can be stored on a single track. A remainder indicates that not all the records could be stored if only the quotient were used; in other words, the product of the quotient and the records per track would be less than the total number of records in the file. By rounding up, we are certain that enough space will be allocated to hold all the records.

What if the data are blocked? Theoretically, less space should be needed, since fewer interrecord gaps are stored. Let's see if the theory works. We'll try a *blocking factor* of ten, meaning that ten logical records will be grouped to form one physical record. The physical record length is 710 characters. Plug the new block length into the formula described above: 135 + 710 is 845. The capacity of a track is still 13,030 bytes, so 15 physical records will fit on each. Remember, however, that a physical record holds 10 logical records. That's 150 logical records per track. Only 34 tracks are needed to hold all the data. By blocking the data, the required space has been reduced from 80 to 34 tracks, and that's significant.

In general, increasing the blocking factor reduces the amount of space required to hold the data. Figure M.6 shows the IBM 3330 space required by the year-to-date file using a variety of blocking factors. Initially, the impact of additional blocking is dramatic, but note how the curve soon begins to level out. The analyst should pick a blocking factor that lies near the beginning of the horizontal portion of the curve; in this example, 14 might make sense.

Note that the curve of Fig. M.6 is not quite smooth; for example, as the blocking factor goes from 9, to 10, to 11, the number of tracks goes from 33, to 34, and back to 33 again. Why? This phenomenon results from using integer arithmetic in computing records per track. For example, imagine that the logical record length were 638 bytes. A blocking factor of ten yields a physical record of 6380 bytes; using the formula above, we would add 135 to get 6515 positions per physical record. The track capacity is 13,030 bytes, so exactly two physical records (twenty logical records) could be stored on each track. Increase the blocking factor to eleven. The physical record length would now be 7018 bytes, but only one such record would fit on a 13,030 byte track. In this example, increasing the blocking factor from ten to eleven reduced the number of logical records per track from twenty to eleven. The analyst should be aware that this happens—more is not always better. A good idea is to write a quick BASIC program to compute space requirements for a variety of blocking factors.

What if keys are used? Another gap (more overhead) and the key length must be added to the overhead and record length described above, and thus the formula (for an IBM 3330) becomes:

138

Blocking Factor	Number of Tracks
1	80
2	54
3	46
4	41
5	38
6	37
7	34
8	33
9	33
10	34
11	33
12	33
13	33
14	30
15	31
16	32
17	30
18	31
19	30
20	32
21	30
22	29
23	31
24	30
25	29

Fig. M.6: *Disk space as a function of the blocking factor.*

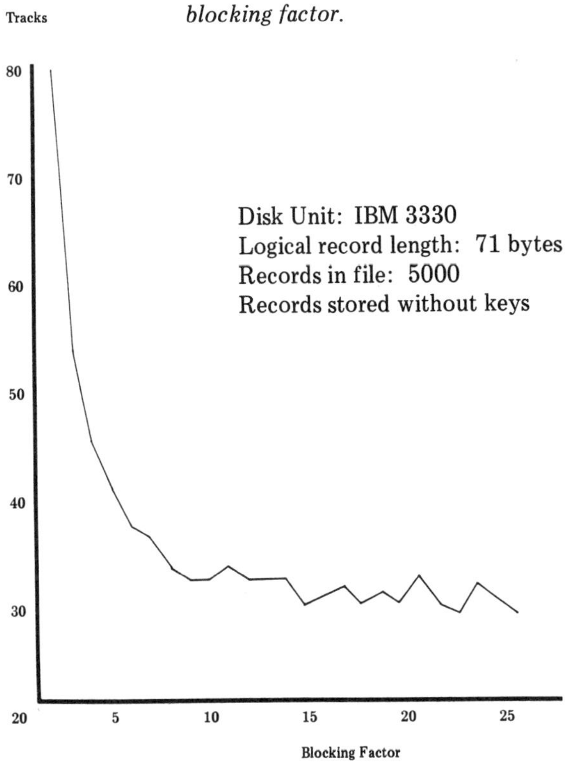

Tracks

Disk Unit: IBM 3330
Logical record length: 71 bytes
Records in file: 5000
Records stored without keys

Blocking Factor

space/record = 135 + 56 + key length + data length

As an exercise, repeat the calculations using this new formula.

The analyst should consider other factors, too. For example, when an indexed file is used, the index or indexes must be stored, and space must be allocated to store them. Overflow space is also easy to overlook. Many direct access techniques generate *synonyms*, two or more records that randomize to the same physical disk address. It is impossible to store two or more records in the same space; when synonyms occur, the subsequent records must be placed on an overflow area. If overflow is a possibility, the analyst must allocate space for it.

Is there anything the analyst can do to squeeze the same amount of data into even less space? Why not shrink some of the fields? For example, computational fields such as the year-to-date gross pay and the other year-to-date statistics can be stored in numeric rather than in character or display form. If each of the seven-digit numbers in Fig. M.1 were stored as a four-byte packed decimal or BCD field, the logical record length would drop from seventy-one to fifty-three bytes. Recompute the space requirements for the year-to-date file using this new logical record length.

139

Codes can sometimes be used, too. For example, in an accounts receivable file, a one-character code might be used instead of a four- or five-digit credit limit, thus saving three or four bytes per record. Be careful when using codes, however. Outside of the system that uses them, they are meaningless. It is possible to create so much confusion by using a code that the apparent savings are lost to increased programming and user costs. Don't forget that the objective of file design is minimizing the total cost of the file, not just the physical storage cost.

In the examples presented above, the IBM 3330 and a 256-byte sector were used as illustrations. Other disk units may differ. The analyst should identify the proper formulas or sector size for his or her own installation.

REFERENCES

1. Davis, William S. (1983). *Operating Systems: a Systematic View.* Reading, Massachusetts: Addison-Wesley Publishing Company.

2. IBM Corporation (1974). *Introduction to IBM Direct-Access Storage Devices and Organization Methods.* White Plains, New York: IBM Corporation. Publication number GC20-1649.

3. Lewis, T.G. and Smith (1976). *Applying Data Structures.* Boston: Houghton Mifflin Company.

Module N

Forms Design
and Report Design

OUTLINE

COMMUNICATING WITH PEOPLE

The basic function of a computer is to process data into information. Most systems involve people; ultimately, they provide the data and use the information. In this module, we will consider three basic media for communicating with people: printed reports, data collection forms, and CRT screens.

A printed report is an output medium. It provides a permanent, inexpensive, portable copy of large volumes of data, but the information is static, and it can quickly become outdated. An alternative is displaying information on a CRT terminal. CRTs are fast, and the information displayed is current. Unfortunately, the display is also temporary, not very portable, and limited in volume. Clearly, the analyst faces a tradeoff in choosing between reports and displays.

Data collection forms are used to capture input data. Forms are inexpensive and, if properly designed, can be used by almost anyone. They are, however, difficult to process. They must be handled and/or transcribed by human clerks, and this is both expensive and error-prone. Using such techniques as OCR, mark sense, and MICR, machine-readable forms can be designed, but these techniques limit the flexibility of the forms. For many applications, a CRT terminal is an alternative. Screens are flexible—they can be used to collect almost any kind of data. Once data are entered through a terminal, they can be stored in machine-readable form; no additional handling is required. However, CRT terminals are relatively expensive, and users require at least a minimum level of training. Once again, we face a tradeoff.

Once a medium is selected, how does an analyst design an appropriate report, data entry form, or CRT screen? While certainly not complete, the material below suggests a number of guidelines.

REPORT DESIGN

The basic work document for designing a report is a printer spacing chart (Fig. N.1). The chart is simply a grid, with each block representing one print position. Using it, the analyst describes, line by line and print position by print position, the structure of a report. Eventually, the analyst or a programmer converts each line on the printer spacing chart to an appropriate set of source language constants or to a data structure.

The report outlined in Fig. N.1 contains headers, detail lines, and summary lines. Page or topic headers identify the report; they are printed at the top of each page or following a major control break. The report date should always be included, and page numbers are helpful, too. Column headers identify the data elements listed in a report, and must be coordinated with the detailed data; more about this later. Headers should clearly describe the report and its contents to the target audience. For example, technical people tend to use acronyms and abbreviations which, while quite reasonable on a technical report, would be inappropriate on one designed for management or the general public. User groups have their own shorthands, too; for example, YTD may be an acceptable abbreviation for "year-to-date" if the target audience is payroll clerks or accountants, but other groups might not assume that meaning.

Fig. N.1: *A mock-up of a typical report on a printer spacing chart.*

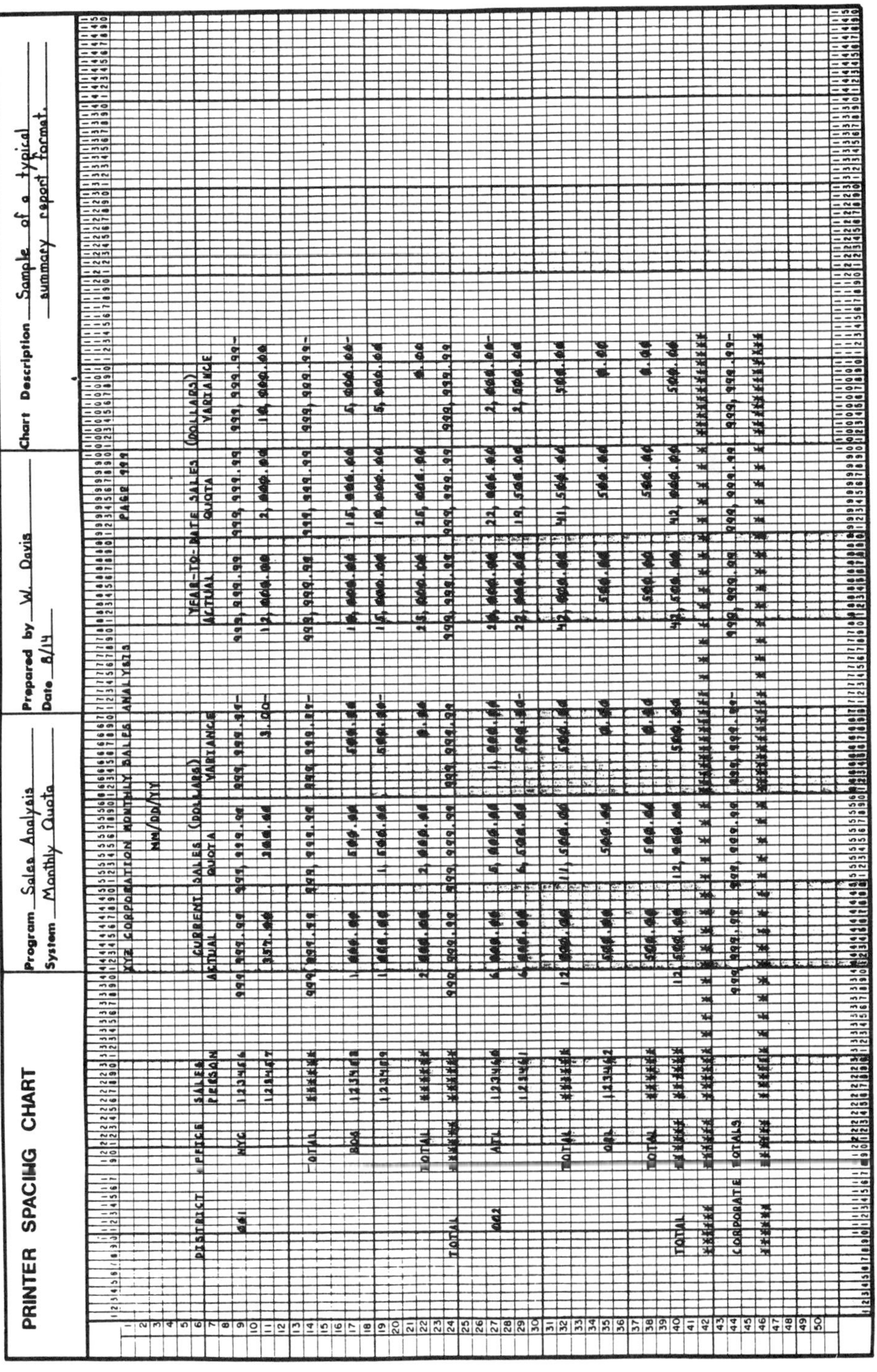

As the name implies, a detail line provides detailed data. The process of designing a report begins here. First, list all the data elements or fields to be included in the report. Group related items; for example, Fig. N.1 shows three clear groupings: identification, current sales, and year-to-date sales. Next, define the number of print positions needed for each element by writing its maximum and/or minimum value; include appropriate punctuation and a sign. For non-numeric items, use the field length.

The column headers are planned next. Write each header beside the maximum/minimum value of the associated data element. If the header is wider than the data, then it defines the column width; for example, in Fig. N.1, the first report column, DISTRICT, is eight positions wide because the header requires eight positions. Otherwise, the data element determines the column width; for example, consider the fourth column, ACTUAL.

Is there enough space to print the complete report? Add the maximum column widths. Remember that there must be at least one space between columns, so count the number of columns, add one (for the left margin), and add this count to the sum of the column widths. Is the total less than or equal to the printer's line width (common widths are 80, 120, and 132 positions)? If not, it may be necessary to delete fields or change headers.

Given the list of fields, their associated headers, and the maximum column widths, the report format can be layed out. Spaces should be left between columns. How many? There is no easy answer. The objective is to produce a report that is easy to read. The only way to determine if a report layout is good is to lay it out and look at it; if it looks good, it probably is. A few suggestions can be made, however. Related items should be grouped; for example, on Fig. N.1, extra space separates the three logical groupings described above. Wider margins should be left on both sides of the paper, and at the top and bottom; people expect margins around printed material. Finally, key fields should be strategically placed; for example, the most significant field on the report outlined in Fig. N.1 is probably the variance (the difference between actual sales and the quota), so this field is placed near the right margin, where negative signs are visually obvious. Key data elements might be further highlighted; for example, the words "BEHIND QUOTA" might be printed to the right of a detail line associated with a sales person who is significantly behind quota.

Avoid printing repetitive data. For example, consider the district identification code in Fig. N.1. Within a district are several sales offices; within each office are several sales people. Should the district identification code be printed on each detail line? No; it should appear only on the first line for a district. Why? Consider the partial report illustrated in Fig. N.2. Which version is easier to read? Note how the version on the right clearly shows which offices belong to which district. Repeating the same descriptive data generates needless clutter, and interferes with the clarity of a report.

What about the summary lines? They should be offset or highlighted in some way. Note how, in Fig. N.1, we have printed the word "TOTAL" in the appropriate column and skipped an extra line before and after each summary line. Key totals might be boxed, and asterisks are commonly used to visually mark key summary lines.

Fig. N.2: *A partial report illustrating the value of suppressing repetitive information.*

a. **With repetitive data displayed.**   b. **With repetitive data suppressed.**

DISTRICT	OFFICE		DISTRICT	OFFICE
001	NYC		001	NYC
001	BOS			BOS
001	PHL			PHL
001	WAS			WAS
002	ATL		002	ATL
002	ORL			ORL
002	DAL			DAL
002	HOU			HOU
003	CHI		003	CHI
003	STL			ATL
003	MSP			MSP
003	KC			KC
004	LA		004	LA
004	SF			SF
004	SEA			SEA
004	ANC			ANC

The objective is to create a report that clearly conveys the necessary information. There is an acid test—can the intended audience read it? There is only one way to find out—ask. A printer spacing chart should be used to prepare a mock-up of a report, and this mock-up should be reviewed by the intended audience. If the people who must use a report have trouble reading it, the fault is probably not theirs, and the report should be redesigned.

FORMS DESIGN

A report provides output information to people; a form is designed to collect input data from people. To an extent, a form can be viewed as a report with blank spaces to be filled in; thus, many of the suggestions made under report design apply to forms design, too. Once collected, however, the data will have to be entered into the computer, and the analyst must take this eventual end use into account.

Some applications call for free-form data entry, while others demand that the data be rigidly structured. A key variable is the expected data volume. Designing a form is independent of the volume; however, the costs of collecting, entering, and processing the data increase as the volume increases. Unstructured forms are easy to design; to cite an extreme example, a tape recorder might be an acceptable free-form medium. Unfortunately, free-form data are difficult to enter, and even more difficult to process. It takes time to design a rigidly structured form, but once the form has been designed, data collection, data entry, and processing are greatly simplified. The more rigid the form, the more time it takes to design it. The more free-form the data, the longer it takes to extract and enter them. With relatively little data, it might make sense to use free-form data collection techniques and spend extra time on data entry. With volumes of data, time spent on form design can save a great deal of data entry time.

Often, a standard form—punched cards, test score sheets, MICR documents, OCR forms, UPC forms—can be adapted to a new application. Existing forms are not always suitable, however, and new ones must be created. While a detailed discussion of forms design is beyond the scope of this book, a few suggestions can be offered. One common technique is providing a series of boxes or blanks to be filled in, with headers or labels identifying the data elements to be entered. Another option is a list of possible choices for ticking or circling. Many professional printers distribute sample forms; a quick perusal might suggest an approach. Finally, when in doubt, seek expert advice. Many large organizations employ graphic designers. A smaller firm might contact a local printer; most are more than willing to help in exchange for some business.

How might the data be entered? Some forms—OCR, mark sense, bar-codes—can be read electronically. Others must be transcribed by data entry clerks. Traditionally, data were recorded on coding sheets and then given to a keypunch operator. Today, a more common option is to enter the data through a CRT terminal; often, a mock-up of the form is displayed, and a clerk simply fills in the blanks. What function is performed by the clerk? The data are copied. Copying data is expensive and error-prone. Why not use the CRT terminal as a data *collection* device? We'll consider this option in the next several paragraphs.

SCREEN DESIGN

A CRT terminal can be used for input, output, or both. Some are designed to read and write single lines. On input, each line holds one logical record. Often, such terminals are used much like keypunches, with data simply copied to the screen from coding forms. Conversational data entry is an option. A control program begins by displaying a prompt asking the clerk to enter a specific data element. In response, a value is entered and stored, and the prompt for the next data element displayed. On output, single line terminals are similar to printers; each line represents one line of a report. However, as a screen fills, old information begins to scroll off the top as new information enters from the bottom. This can make a screen difficult to read, and forces the user to work at the screen's pace. Consequently, large reports are rarely output through a screen.

Other CRT terminals perform full screen I/O. Using this approach, the contents of a full screen are defined in a buffer and then displayed. A visible marker called a cursor indicates the position on the screen where the next character typed by the user will appear. Buttons to move the cursor up, down, right, or left are generally available, allowing the user to position the cursor (and thus type) anywhere on the screen. Using full screen I/O, a dummy version of a form can be displayed, and data entered by filling in the blanks.

Look at a screen. Count the number of characters displayed on a single line. Now, count the number of lines. These two numbers define a rectangular grid. For example, the draft of this book was prepared on a personal microcomputer system. The screen displays 25 lines of 80 characters each, and thus can be represented by an 80 by 25 grid. To lay out a screen, start with a sheet of graph paper, and block out a grid pattern equal to the capacity of your CRT. By printing one character per box, labels, headers, and data elements can be positioned, and the contents of the screen planned; the process is similar to defining a report format.

Several techniques can be used to highlight key data elements or to distinguish names, labels, and data. A simple approach is to use upper case for names and labels, and lower case for data. With more sophisticated terminals, different colors or reverse video can be used. Blinking characters or fields seem almost to jump out from the screen, and boxes or arrows are almost as effective.

Computer graphics is a developing technology. Space does not permit a detailed explanation of graphic techniques; the interested student might consider the book by Foley and Van Dam referenced at the end of this module. Touch sensitive screens and graphic input are other technologies of the near future. A good course in computer graphics is strongly recommended.

REFERENCES

1. Fitzgerald, Jerry, Fitzgerald, and Stallings (1981). *Fundamentals of Systems Analysis*, Second Edition. New York: John Wiley & Sons.

2. Foley, James D. and Van Dam (1982). *Fundamentals of Interactive Computer Graphics*. Reading, Massachusetss: Addison-Wesley Publishing Company.

3. Gore, Marvin and Stubbe (1979). *Elements of Systems Analysis for Business Data Processing*. Dubuque, Iowa: Wm. C. Brown.

4. Parkin, Andrew (1980). *Systems Analysis*. Cambridge, Massachusetts: Winthrop Publishers, Inc.

Module O

Decision Tables and Decision Trees

OUTLINE

PROCESSES WITH MULTIPLE NESTED DECISIONS

Algorithms involving multiple nested decisions are difficult to describe using structured English (Module H), pseudocode (Module I), or logic flowcharts (Module J). In this module, two alternative tools, decision tables and decision trees, are introduced. We'll use a simple example to illustrate both: Assume that the basketball coach has asked us to look through the student records and produce a list of all full-time male students who are at least 6 feet 5 inches tall and who weigh at least 180 pounds. First, we'll consider decision tables.

DECISION TABLES

A sample decision table is shown as Fig. O.1. It is divided into four sections: a condition stub at the upper left, a condition entry at the upper right, an action stub at the lower left, and an action entry at the lower right. The questions are listed in the condition stub; note that each requires a yes/no response. The associated actions are listed in the action stub. The responses (Y or N) are recorded in the condition entry, while the appropriate action is indicated in the action entry.

Perhaps the easiest way to understand a decision table is to read one. Let's begin with the first question: Is the student male? There are two possible answers: yes (Y) or no (N). What if the answer is yes; can we make a decision? Not yet; three more tests must be passed. What if the answer is no? If the student is not male, she is not a candidate for the basketball team, and thus can be rejected. Move down the column containing the N, and note the X on the action entry line following "Reject the student."

FIG. O.1: *A decision table for the basketball problem.*

Condition Stub:	Condition Entry:				
Is the student male?	Y	N			
Is the student taking at least 12 credit hours?	Y		N		
Is the student at least 77 inches tall?	Y			N	
Does the student weigh at least 180 pounds?	Y				N
Action Stub:	Action Entry:				
List the student's name and address	X				
Reject the student.		X	X	X	X

Move on to the second question: Is the student taking at least 12 credit hours? Again, there are two possible answers: yes or no. Note how the answers are recorded on Fig. O.1. The second Y is directly under the first one; this implies that the answers to both questions must be yes before the action identified by an X in that column's action entry can be taken. Is a yes response to both questions sufficient? No; two more tests remain. What if the answer to this second question is no, however? The student can be rejected. Why isn't the second N aligned under the first one? Because any single N, by itself, is enough to reject the student.

Read the rest of the table. It clearly shows that the student's name and address will be listed only if the answers to all four questions are yes, but that the student will be rejected if the answer to any one is no. When an algorithm involves more than two or three nested decisions, a decision table gives a clear and concise picture of the logic.

DECISION TREES

As an alternative, the analyst might use a decision science or management science tool called a decision tree. Let's consider the general structure of this tool, and then discuss how it might be applied to systems analysis and design. Imagine that you have an opportunity to purchase, for $50,000, exclusive rights to market a new product, magnetic soap. If the product catches on, you stand to make a great deal of money. On the other hand, magnetic soap might flop, and you could lose your entire investment.

The decision tree of Fig. O.2 is a graphic representation of this problem. The tree starts (on the left) with an *act fork*, represented by a small box. Emanating from it are two branches; they represent your possible decisions; buy or don't buy the rights. Move along the "buy" branch. The dot represents an *event fork*. Coming from it are two more branches representing the consequences of this decision—perhaps the product will be successful; perhaps it won't. Each branch terminates in an *outcome*.

Fig. O.2:   *A simple decision tree.*

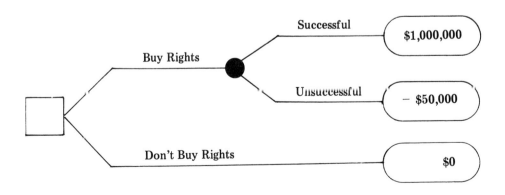

151

Fig. O.3: *A decision tree for the basketball problem.*

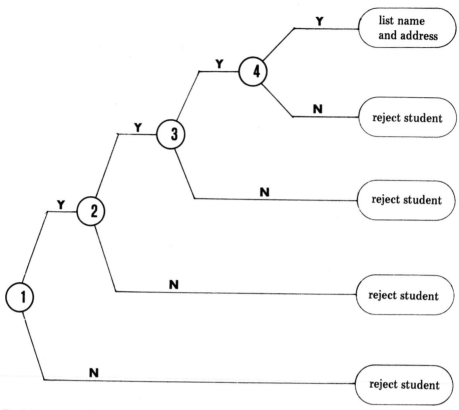

Decisions:

1. Is the student male?

2. Is the student taking at least 12 hours?

3. Is the student at least 77 inches tall?

4. Does the student weigh at least 180 pounds?

If the product is successful, you stand to make a million dollars. If it fails, you lose $50,000. Go back to the act fork. Before the decision is made, you have an option not to buy the rights. Clearly, this decision will cost you nothing. There are no consequences associated with this choice, either; your outcome is zero whether magnetic soap catches on or not.

The decision tree is a graphic representation of the decision, events, and consequences associated with a problem. Once the tree is drawn, probabilities can be associated with each branch, and expected values of the outcomes computed. Interested students may find decision trees excellent for illustrating alternative system strategies; the text referenced at the end of this module is a good source. We are, however, more interested in using decision trees to graphically represent nested decision logic.

Let's return to the basketball problem. The algorithm consists of a series of four nested questions or decisions; Fig. O.3 is a decision tree for this logic. Each question or decision is represented as a circle. Begin with the first one: Is the student male? There are two possible responses: yes or no. If the answer is no, the student is rejected; a yes answer, on the other hand, leads to another question. Again, there are two possible answers: yes and no. Again, a no leads to an outcome: reject the student, while a yes response leads to yet another question. Follow each branch on the tree to its logical outcome. Can you see how a student's name and address are listed only if all four questions are answered affirmatively? Decision trees are easy to construct, and graphically illustrate decision logic.

As we mentioned earlier, once a decision tree is drawn, probabilities can be associated with each branch, and the expected values of the outcomes computed. The systems analyst can take advantage of this basic idea to improve the efficiency of an algorithm without affecting its clarity. Consider the basketball problem. Imagine that you have one hundred student records to check. The first question asks if the student is male. How many students are eliminated by this first question? Probably, about half; we would expect about fifty of the one hundred students to be male. Consequently, the second criterion, credit hours, is checked for fifty students. How many are taking twelve hours or more? On some campuses, most of them; on others, very few; let's assume forty of the fifty are full-time. Student height is thus checked for forty students; how many exceed the height limit? Very few; perhaps three or four are checked for weight. Consider the total number of tests performed—100, plus 50, plus 40, plus 3 or 4 is over 190 decisions.

Change the sequence of the tests. Which of the four questions is likely to eliminate the most students? Relatively few will be 77 inches tall or taller; thus height is a good first screen. After one hundred records are checked for student height, how many will remain? Perhaps five or six. Thus, only five or six records are checked for the other criteria; consequently, the total number of tests is reduced. In general, when designing a nested decision algorithm, the most discriminating tests should be performed first. The result is improved program efficiency at little or no cost.

REFERENCES

1. Brown, Rex V., Kahr, and Peterson (1974). *Decision Analysis for the Manager.* New York: Holt, Rinehart and Winston.

Module P

Data Base Management

OUTLINE

155

THE CUSTOMIZED FILE APPROACH

Payroll was, for many firms, one of the very first computer applications. The reason for using a computer to do payroll is easy to pinpoint. As the firm grows, the personnel time (and thus cost) of processing payroll grows, and it doesn't take too much imagination to see that by automating this highly repetitive task and doing it on a computer, these costs can be brought under control. Payroll is easy to cost justify. Other early computer applications—accounting, ledgers, accounts payable, accounts receivable, inventory, bill-of-material processing, report generation—are equally easy to cost justify on their own merits. A basic argument in each case is cost reduction: It's less expensive to do the job on a computer than to do it manually.

Most firms believe in cost justifying any new project; if the expected benefits do not outweigh the cost of achieving those benefits, no sense investing the money or personnel. These early computer applications fit beautifully into the cost justification mold, with each single computer application standing on its own. This approach did, however, lead to a method of organizing data which has come back to haunt many companies.

The basic problem begins with the application-by-application approach to developing computer-based systems. Each single application stands on its own, with little or no central planning to provide a context for these applications. As a result, efficiency is defined at the application level. The "ideal" program is one that uses a minimum amount of main memory, a minimum amount of CPU time, and a minimum amount of I/O.

One of the best ways to achieve program-level optimization is to customize the data files to fit the application. Thus a typical organization has a set of payroll files, a set of billing files, a set of accounts payable files, and so on. It is the very independence of these files, the lack of integration of all this information, that creates problems.

Data Redundancy and the Lack of Data Integrity

Perhaps the most obvious problem of the customized file approach is *data redundancy*. With so many independent files, it is almost certain that the same element of data will appear in several different places. For example, consider the files found at a college or university. The chances are that information concerning a given student appears on several different files. For billing purposes, the student's name and address appear on the bursar's records. These same fields are also on the registrar's files, the department-of-major's file, housing files, library files, alumni files, automobile registration files, and probably several others. What happens if an address (or name) changes? The correction will be made on some of the files, perhaps even most of the files, but the chances are that the correction will not be made on *all* the files. Thus there will be two (or more) different versions of the same data element. When two or more values exist for the same element of data, the *integrity* of that data is subject to question. With different versions of the "truth," how can we trust the data?

Data Ownership

Individual users tend to define data integrity strictly in terms of their own application. The bursar's office will take steps to ensure that the financial data are accurate. The registrar will carefully verify academic data. Each user is concerned with the integrity of the data that are relevant to that user's application. One way to guarantee the integrity of a given file is to limit access to that file. Thus the bursar's files are available only to the bursar's office; by denying others access, the risk of incorrect data being introduced by an untrained individual is minimized. Another factor is security; the bursar's records contain certain highly confidential information, and limiting access helps to preserve this confidentiality. The reasons for denying access to data are many, and they are easy to justify. Such a localized, "this application" definition of data integrity does, however, lead to another problem.

Who *owns* the data? The answer is not always clear. Operations controls the hardware on which the data are stored; thus operations has a legitimate claim. Without software to create, maintain, and manipulate the data on the files, there would be no files; thus systems and programming might claim ownership. The user, on the other hand, is responsible for the integrity of the data, and thus has the right to define the conditions for data access. All three groups—operations, systems and programming, and the user—can reasonably claim ownership. Split responsibility never works very well.

To access a given file, it is often necessary to get the approval of the user, computer operations, and the programmers. The result is red tape and bureaucracy: the "Mother, may I?" problem. The bursar may have the most accurate file of student names and addresses but because the bursar's records contain other, confidential information, no one else is allowed to access these records. The result is the creation of other files containing the same information, redundant data. This takes time, and costs money. The fact that data exist on the computer does not necessarily mean that they are easily accessible. Customized files tend to limit *data accessibility*.

Data-Dependent Programs

Programs designed to access custom files are *data-dependent*. Consider, for example, the standard master file update application. Two files, a master file and a transactions file are input to this program, which matches the transactions to the appropriate master file record and creates a new master file. Much of the logic of the program is concerned with input and output. To the user, such problems as matching records, first record processing, and last record processing are irrelevant. All the user really wants are the results in the form of valid pay checks or bills. The programmer is really solving two problems: the user's data manipulation problem and the problem of moving data between primary and secondary storage. If the structure or organization of the data changes, the standard master file update program will not work. The program is clearly data-dependent.

Often data dependency is more subtle. Consider, for example, the problem of how dates are stored on many customized files. To save space (remember, space minimization is one of the objectives of this approach), the year is often stored as a two-digit number—84 rather than 1984. Imagine a program that ages inventory, compiling statistics on stock that is over 90 days old, from 60 to 90 days old, and so on. The logic of this program would involve a comparison with the current date. What happens on January 1, 2000? The two-digit year is 00. Does 85 mean 15 years in the past or 85 years in the future? Beginning on January 1, 2000, any logic based on a comparison with the current date will not work!

Why not simply change the date field to hold a four-digit year? Because hundreds of programs have already been written to expect a two-digit date, and they would all have to be changed. As if that is not enough, hundreds of other programs that do not even reference the date in their logic do read a record that contains the date. Changing from two to four digits means a change in the logical record length. The result: *every* program that even reads a record containing the date would have to be changed, whether that program used the date or not. Clearly, all these programs are data-dependent.

Whenever a data file is customized to meet the needs of a particular program, that program, in turn, becomes locked to its data. Any change in data content, data structure, or file organization can imply a need to modify the program. As a result, management is often faced with three almost equally unacceptable choices: (1) patch the present system, (2) write a new system from scratch, or (3) risk falling behind the competition. Simple maintenance becomes impossible because such a significant portion of the program is locked to the physical structure of its custom files.

Actually, all the programmer really wants is a set of values for certain data elements that are relevant to the logic of a program. The details associated with physically retrieving that data—the file organization, the job control language, the special parameters on the I/O macros—are really secondary. In fact, a surprising number of programmers really do not understand these details; they just use them, by rote. Although it is difficult to identify the precise cost of this data dependency, it may well be greater than data redundancy, the lack of data integrity, and the problem with data accessibility combined.

How might we solve these problems? Increasingly, it appears that data base management might be the answer.

THE CENTRAL DATA BASE CONCEPT

Most of the problems cited above were a direct result of the traditional approach to developing computer applications, one at a time, with no coordination or central planning. The big problem was seen to be the customized file, with its data integrity, data ownership, and data dependency implications.

Why not group all of an organization's data resources to form a large, integrated *central data base*? To control access to this data base, we might provide a *data base management system* and require all input and output operations to flow through this software module. The result could well be a solution to many of the data access problems cited above. Clearly, with a single, centralized data base, the problems of data redundancy and data integrity would be minimized. Centralized data implies centralized control, thus solving the data ownership problem. With all programs accessing a common data base, any changes in the physical structure of the data would impact only the data base manager; the application programs could be relatively data independent. Let's investigate how the central data base concept might help to solve each of these problems.

Data Integrity

On a centralized data base, we would store a single version of each *element* of data. A school, for example, might store a student's name and address on the data base. Any application requiring the student name and address would get it from this central source. With a data base, if a given student's name or address were to change, it would be corrected once, on the data base, and everyone would have the correct information.

Clearly, the idea of a central data base almost eliminates the problem of data redundancy. Redundant data are data that are stored in several different places. The data base concept implies that an element of data will be stored once, in the central data base. Reduced data redundancy means improved data accuracy.

Another factor that would tend to improve the accuracy of data on a data base is ease of verification. With multiple, customized files, the user department might be held responsible for editing or verifying input data, at a *record* level. Certain critical fields would, we might expect, be carefully scrutinized, but other fields less critical to the application would receive less careful consideration. This is one reason why different values often exist for redundant data fields. With a data base, the department or user group most concerned with the accuracy of a given data element can be assigned verification responsibility for that *field*, and no group would have to be concerned with the accuracy of data elements of secondary importance. Key department verification of *each* individual data element would lead to much greater data integrity.

Reducing data redundancy and clearly defining responsibility for the accuracy of each data element will tend to improve data integrity. Earlier, we saw that one way to help ensure the integrity of a particular customized file was to limit access to that file. Often, the justification was the confidential nature of one or more fields in a record. A key feature of the central data base approach is a data base management system lying between the application program and the data base. With this module in place, *all* access to the data base can be routed through a common control mechanism. Security, at the field or data element level, can be implemented in the data base management system. With this kind of control, a given application program can be restricted to authorized data elements only. Security is no longer an excuse for denying data access.

Data Ownership

Another direct result of the central data base approach is a very clear definition of data ownership. With all of the organization's data collected into a single central data base, it becomes relatively easy to define the data as an *organizational resource*, owned by the *entire* organization. In fact, in today's increasingly complex world, information may well be the organization's most valuable resource.

How might we achieve the objective of clearly defining data ownership? Let's begin with pre-data base, customized files. The Information Management function of most large organizations using this approach will probably resemble Fig. P.1. Reporting to the MIS manager are two functional groups. *Operations* is responsible for the hardware, performing such functions as operating the computers, maintaining the hardware, and entering the data. *Systems and programming* is responsible for planning, implementing, and maintaining the software. Who is responsible for the data? *Physical data*

Fig. P.1: *The pre-data base structure of the MIS function.*

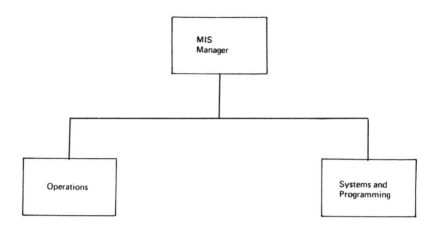

responsibility goes to operations—it owns the hardware on which the data are stored. *Logical* data responsibility belongs to systems and programming—it writes the programs that create and maintain the data. Who is responsible for data integrity? Often, the user. Thus we have a split responsibility and split control. The result is the "Mother, may I?" problem described earlier.

With the data resources centralized, centralized control suddenly becomes possible. Many organizations have restructured their MIS function (Fig. P.2), adding a new department, the *data base administrator* or *DBA*. Operations is still responsible for the hardware, and systems and programming still controls software. The data base administrator controls the data. What are the three primary elements of *any* computer system? Hardware, software, and data. With this new organizational structure, the primary responsibility for each of these major system elements is clearly and unambiguously defined.

Centralized control, unfortunately, carries a certain risk. An unconstrained data base administrator could arbitrarily limit access to the organization's data, becoming a data czar. This is where the data base management system comes into play (Fig. P.3). The data base management system is a software module that lies between the application program and the data base. The rules for accessing the data base are implemented in the data base management system. The task of the data base administrator is thus one of seeing that the rules for data base access, as defined by company policy, are accurately reflected in the data base management system.

Security precautions provide a good example. Because every attempt to access the data base must pass through the data base management system, security rules can be implemented in this software module. Before a given program is allowed to access a particular element of data, the security level of the application can be compared with the security level of the data element, and the request either honored or denied. For

Fig. P.2: *The structure of the MIS function when the centralized data base approach is used.*

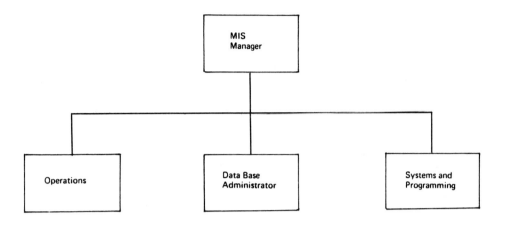

Fig. P.3: *The data base management software comes between the application program and the data base.*

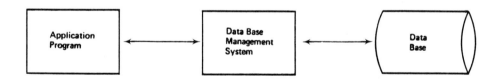

example, a first-level manager might be allowed to access personnel data on his or her employees, but details on higher-level managers might be off-limits.

It seems almost a paradox, but the tighter, more centralized control made possible by the data base approach leads to greater *data accessibility*. With security in place, confidentiality is no longer an excuse for denying access to the data. With improved data integrity, the "we can't trust their data" problem disappears. Suddenly it becomes possible to honor unanticipated requests for information. In fact, many data base systems have implemented *query languages* that allow nontechnical users to extract information from a data base using Englishlike questions. Another popular option is *report generator* software which allows the nontechnical user to structure and actually execute simple one-time programs to generate special-purpose reports from the data base.

161

Data-Independent Programs

The problems of data integrity and data ownership are quite apparent to the computer professional. (Ask any programmer if he or she has ever had to program around a political roadblock, or if different values of what should be the same data element ever appear.) The problem of data dependency is a bit more subtle. As we saw earlier, the programmer using customized files is really solving two problems: data access *and* the user's application. Unfortunately, the programmer rarely sees these two problems as independent—data access and the user's application are so tightly linked that they become a single problem in the programmer's mind and in the code. This is why, when the file organization changes, it is so often necessary to rewrite rather than maintain the program. Programmers do *not* view such rewrites as maintenance. Instead, such projects are seen as new system development.

Management takes a somewhat different view. If an organization has an existing system to generate valid pay checks, and a change in the law makes a new payroll system necessary, programming sees a need for a development project. Management, on the other hand, sees a considerable sum of money being spent to allow the organization to continue doing what it already was doing—generating valid paychecks. Management sees a need for the maintenance of an existing system, and (quite correctly) sees the need to redesign and recode the entire payroll system as highly inefficient. The argument that a change in data structure makes the logic of the existing program totally obsolete is not particularly impressive to nontechnical management. Computer professionals, all too often, are so close to the data dependency problem that they cannot see it.

How might a centralized data base help to make application programs data independent? Consider, once again, a pre-data base application. The programmer requests logical I/O (Fig. P.4) by transferring control to an access method. The access method converts this logical I/O request to a physical I/O request and passes this request to the operating system, which issues the instructions needed to control the physical I/O. The key problem with this approach is that the programmer's "logical" *record* must physically exist somewhere; in other words, if the employee's name and address are required, the programmer must read a record *containing* the name and address. Fields such as name and address simply do not exist independent of that record; the record defines a structure; the record defines the context in which the desired data elements can be found.

With the centralized data base approach, a data base management system is placed between the application program and the access method (Fig. P.5). The data base management system still uses the standard access methods, and still accesses the data base through the operating system, but the application program is insulated from this linkage. The application program can now request true logical I/O. For example, if the program needs an employee's name and address, only the name and address would be requested from the data base management system. This software package would translate the application program's request for values for these two data elements into the necessary record requests, issue the necessary traditional I/O operation or operations, accept the input data records, extract the relevant field or data element values, and pass them back to the application program. Thus the programmer could ignore the details of physical I/O.

Fig. P.4: *Without a data base management system, the programmer codes logical record-level I/O.*

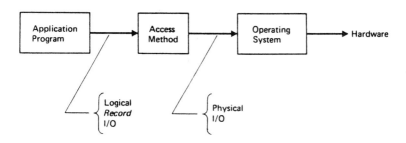

Fig. P.5: *With a data base management system, the programmer can code logical data element-level I/O.*

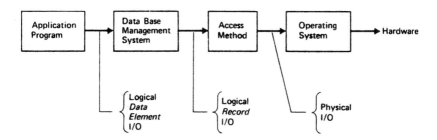

Consider very carefully the distinction between traditional logical I/O and true logical I/O. When a programmer reads a traditional record from a traditional file using a traditional access method, that record must physically exist. The data might be stored as a large physical record composed of several logical records. A large logical record might be spread over two or more physical records. The point is that the logical record holds the data in a fixed structure, and when the programmer requests a logical record, the entire record will be transferred into (or out from) the program. The fact that the programmer may not need every field in that logical record is not relevant; the record's structure within the computer will be identical to the record's structure on the external, physical storage device. Using the traditional approach, the programmer must accept the entire record as it is physically stored, or accept none of it.

A data base management system supports true logical I/O. If the programmer needs only certain data elements, the programmer can create a logical record or data structure that contains only those data elements. The data base management system accepts the programmer's request for data, issues the necessary physical I/O commands, and assembles the data elements requested by the programmer. It is possible that the programmer's request may match the physical structure of the data on the external device. More often, however, the logical record requested by the programmer does not physically exist until the data base management system assembles the pieces. Thus the programmer can ignore the physical structure of the data.

What if the physical organization of the data were to change? Since the application programs are not concerned with the physical organization of the data, they will not be affected. Rather than modifying hundreds of different programs, the new data structure could be implemented by modifying only one: the data base management system. This is what we mean by the term data-independence.

The idea of data independency is an *extremely* important concept, especially to the future computer professional. It directly influences programmer productivity, a key concern of management in these days when the demand for programmers is much greater than the supply. Increasingly, the attitude of both management and technical people is changing. The emphasis is shifting away from *computer* efficiency (with its implied concentration on the machine) and toward problem solving (with a concentration on meeting user requirements). This trend will have a profound impact on the job of the future systems analyst or programmer.

The Central Data Base: Advantages

Let's briefly summarize the advantages derived from the central data base approach. First, perhaps most importantly, applications can be relatively data-independent; the programmer can ignore the physical structure of the data. Second, data responsibility and authority are clearly defined, often in the person of a data base administrator. Finally, data integrity is improved through reduced data redundancy, better data verification and control, and better security. The result of all these factors is that the data resources of the organization are accessible to the entire organization.

The Central Data Base: Disadvantages

No improvement is without its cost, and data base management is no exception. Concerns range from the overhead associated with the data base, through the impact of the data base approach on the programmer, and on to the cost of the data base itself.

The data base management system is positioned between the application program and the traditional access methods. Speaking positively, the data base approach insulates the application program from the data, thus promoting data independence. From a more negative perspective, the use of a data base represents one more level of overhead. Rather than communicating directly with the access method, the program must now go through the data base management system. Overhead implies execution time and memory space. There is little question that a well-written program accessing customized files will run faster than a well-written program performing the same data processing functions but accessing its data through a data base management system.

The basic problem with this argument is that it tends to define efficiency in primarily hardware terms. The objective of the organization is not to minimize the cost of running payroll on the computer. The objective of the organization (with respect to payroll) might be better stated as minimize the total, long-run costs of producing valid paychecks. The total cost would certainly include the on-the-computer costs of concern to the single application people, but other costs would be considered as well—for example, coding costs and long-term program maintenance costs. Of even greater concern is the relationship between the payroll application and the organization's other information processing needs. From a total organization point of view, the "efficiency" argument loses a great deal of its appeal.

By insulating the programmer from the need to worry about I/O, the use of data base management techniques does tend to simplify the coding process. From a management perspective, this is clearly a positive result, with implications for improved programmer productivity. To the programmer, the impact of data base management often seems negative. By simplifying the task of writing code, the use of data base management makes the job of the programmer seem more mundane. Programmers complain about the loss of an opportunity to exercise their creativity. Some choose to leave the organization, moving to firms that provide more of a technical challenge. In these days of high demand for programmers, the organization must consider this risk.

Actually, there is more to programming than writing code. In fact, excessive concentration on the "neat" technical details may be one reason why programmers have historically had such a difficult time communicating with their users. Data base management does not impact the portion of a program concerned with actually solving the user's needs; it impacts that part of the program that is concerned with I/O. In other words, from a management perspective, the alleged impact of data base management on programmer creativity affects a secondary function, I/O, and does not affect the primary function of the program. We still need creative people to translate user needs into technical terms, but must that creativity be extended to the details of file manipulation? Perhaps what we really need at this level is *precision*, and not creativity Frankly, except for the implied "I'll take my marbles and go home" threat of programmers who know they are in short supply, the creativity argument is irrelevant.

There is, however, one very strong argument against the data base approach—cost. The data base management system, that critical software package, is a very complex program that is beyond the capabilities of most installations. Commercial data base management systems can be purchased or leased, but they are quite expensive. The cost of developing or leasing and installing a data base management system can easily hit $50,000 or more.

The cost of the control software is insignificant when it is compared to the cost of developing the data base, however. In a relatively brief period of time, all the data stored in hundreds of previously customized files must be merged to form the data base. The application programs, perhaps hundreds of them, that accessed the customized files, must be rewritten or modified to access the data base. These phase-over costs can be enormous, perhaps ranging into the hundreds of thousands of dollars.

These costs are concrete. They are short-run costs, representing dollars that must be spent now, rather than at some vague time in the future. Unfortunately, the benefits derived from the central data base approach—data integrity, data availability, and data independent programs—are less concrete and more in the future. Management is asked to spend a great deal of short-run money for a somewhat questionable long-run payoff. Not surprisingly, many organizations have decided not to change.

Unfortunately, the problem will only get worse. Each year, new applications are added, meaning that the switch to data base will cost more next year than this year. A few decades after the end of World War II, the United States with its largely obsolete steel-making facilities, found it very difficult to compete with Germany and Japan and their rebuilt steel plants. To the American steel industry, the cost of upgrading facilities was prohibitive, but so was the cost of *not* upgrading. In the future, the decision to switch from customized files to a data base approach may be viewed in much the same light.

REFERENCES

1. Date, C. J. (1981). *An Introduction to Database Systems*, third edition. Reading, Mass.: Addison-Wesley.

2. Davis, William S. (1983). *Operating Systems: a Systematic View*, second edition. Reading, Mass.: Addison-Wesley.

3. Kroenke, David (1977). *Database Processing*. Chicago: Science Research Associates, Inc.

4. Martin James (1977). *Computer Data-Base Organization*, second edition. Englewood Cliffs, New Jersey: Prentice-Hall, Inc.

Module Q

Structured Systems Analysis and Design

THE SYSTEM LIFE CYCLE

To this point, specific analysis and design tools and techniques have been presented independently. How are they related? How does a professional systems analyst use these tools and techniques? In this module, an overview of the complete systems analysis and design *process* will be presented. The material represents a generalized version of a modern *structured* methodology.

Structured systems analysis and design is keyed to the *system life cycle* (Fig. Q.1). As a system moves from concept to implementation, it must pass through each of these steps. When a structured approach is used, the systems analyst must progress from step to step in a careful, methodical fashion, completing a number of well defined exit criteria for each step. Let's briefly consider this process. In the descriptions that follow, the exit criteria for each step will be mentioned; refer to the appropriate modules for a detailed description of each.

Problem Definition

What is the problem? This is the key question that must be answered during *problem definition*; it makes little sense to try to solve a problem if you don't know what the problem is. Although the need for problem definition may seem obvious, this is perhaps the most frequently bypassed step in the entire systems analysis and design process.

What is the source of the problem definition? Obviously, someone must recognize that a problem exists. Often the user will encounter difficulties and ask for help. Perhaps management will identify an area of poor performance within the user's function; frequently the systems analyst will spot the problem. Initial discussions concerning the problem are often quite informal. Eventually, however, these discussions reach the point where the user, management, and the systems analyst agree: "Yes, we really do have a problem."

Fig. Q.1: *The steps in the system life cycle.*

Problem definition

Feasibility study

Analysis

System design

Detailed design

Implementation

Maintenance

If the problem is judged significant, management and the user may want the analyst to look into it. Once an analyst is assigned, the process undergoes a subtle change. Assigning an analyst implies a commitment of funds; the informal discussions suddenly become a defined project.

The systems analyst's first responsibility is to prepare a written statement of the objectives and the scope of the problem (Fig. Q.2). Based on interviews with management and the user, the analyst writes a brief description of his or her understanding of the problem, and reviews it with both groups, ideally in a joint user/management meeting. People respond to written statements. They ask for clarification; they correct obvious errors or misunderstandings. This is why a clear statement of objectives is so important.

Management (and perhaps the user) is about to commit funds to support the analyst's work. How much will it cost? This is a reasonable question that all too often is not asked until quite late in the system development process. The analyst should provide a rough estimate of the scope of this financial commitment. Clearly, at this early stage, no one can provide an accurate estimate of the final cost of a project, but "ballpark" estimates or "order of magnitude" estimates are certainly possible. The analyst should also be able to provide an accurate assessment of both the cost and the schedule for the next phase in the system life cycle: the feasibility study. These estimates will give management and the user a sense of the scope of the project.

Problem definition can be quite brief, lasting a single day or even less. The intent is to define the objectives and the scope of the proposed system. Communication breakdowns do occur, and it is essential that the user, management, and the systems analyst agree on a general direction very early in the project. A misunderstood problem definition virtually guarantees that the system will fail to solve the problem.

Fig. Q.2: *Problem definition.*

Step	Key Question	Exit Criteria
Problem definition	What is the problem?	Statement of scope and objectives

The Feasibility Study

What exactly is a *feasibility study*? Basically, it is a high level, capsule version of the entire process, intended to answer a number of questions (Fig. Q.3). What is the problem? *Is there a feasibile solution to the problem?* Is the problem even worth solving? The feasibility study should be relatively brief; the task is not to solve the problem, but to gain a sense of its scope. The user will be asked to react to the feasibility study; how else could we be sure that we are attacking the right problem? Management is vitally concerned with the results, as they will be asked to commit funds and personnel based on the feasibility study.

The statement of scope and objectives prepared during problem definition is generally rather vague. Essentially, the analyst promises to investigate (not to solve) a broadly defined problem. During the feasibility study, the problem definition is brought into sharper focus. Specific system objectives are set, and aspects of the problem that will be excluded from the system are clearly identified. As a result, the analyst should be able to estimate the costs and benefits of the system with greater accuracy. A cost/benefit analysis of the proposed system is an important part of the study.

The feasibility study ends with a formal presentation to the user and to management. This presentation marks a crucial decision point in the life of the project. Many projects will die right here; only those promising a significant return on investment should be pursued. Assuming that management approval is granted, the feasibility study represents an excellent model of the systems analyst's understanding of the problem (comparable to the engineer's design sketches), and provides a clear sense of direction for the subsequent development of the system.

Fig. Q.3: *The feasibility study.*

Step	Key Question	Exit Criteria
Feasibility study	Is there a feasibile solution?	Rough cost/benefit analysis System scope and objectives

Analysis

Analysis is a logical process. The objective of this phase is not to actually solve the problem, but to determine exactly *what must be done to solve the problem*. The user knows what must be done, but does not know how to do it. During analysis, the systems analyst works with the user to develop a logical model of the system (Fig. Q.4).

Many systems analysts have a technical background. The temptation of many technically trained people is to move too quickly to program design, to become *prematurely physical*. This temptation must be avoided. The objective, don't forget, is to solve the user's problem. The user knows the problem, and is the analyst's primary source of information at this stage. If the analyst begins talking about programming details, the user may become lost, and unable to contribute. As a result, the analyst may develop a system that fails to solve the problem.

How can an analyst avoid becoming prematurely physical? A structured methodology can help. With a structured approach, specific exit criteria must be completed for each step in the process. The basic objective of the analysis stage is to develop a logical model of the system, using such tools as data flow diagrams, an elementary data dictionary, and rough descriptions of the relevant algorithms. This logical model is subject to review by both the user and management, who must agree that the model does in fact reflect what should be done to solve the problem.

Fig. Q.4: *Analysis.*

Step	Key Question	Exit Criteria
Analysis	What must be done to solve the problem?	Logical model of system Data flow diagram Data dictionary Algorithms

System Design or High-Level Design

Once the analysis stage is completed, the systems analyst knows what must be done. The next step is to determine, in broad outline form, how the problem might be solved. During *system design*, we are beginning to move from the logical to the physical (Fig. Q.5).

Several alternative solutions might be considered. For example, a given system might be implemented by computer or manual means. If a computer is used, the system might be either batch or interactive. We might use traditional data files; a data base is another option. It is important that the analyst avoid simply picking a system implementation and moving on to program design. Once again, the use of a structured methodology can help.

The question to be answered during system design is: *How, in general, should the problem be solved?* The answer to this question is crucial to both the user and the programmer; thus the exit criteria for this phase must be aimed at both groups. Management is particularly concerned about the future direction of the system. Up to this point, the project has involved the time of a few systems analysts (Fig. Q.6), and the cost has been limited. Detailed design may well involve these analysts plus a few more, and the detailed design stage will take longer; thus the costs begin to accelerate. As we move to implementation, programmers, operators, technical writers, and computer time must be committed, and the accumulated cost increases dramatically. To make matters worse, following implementation is a long-range, potentially expensive maintenance commitment. Before management can support the system, they

171

Step	Key Question	Exit Criteria
System design	How, in general, should the problem be solved?	Alternative solutions System flow diagrams Cost/benefit analysis

Fig. Q.6: *The cost of the system as we move from phase to phase.*

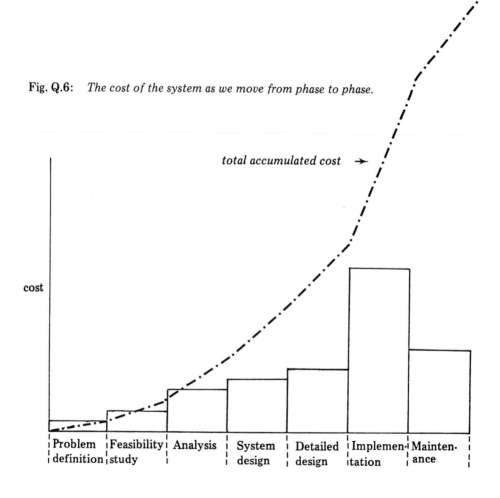

total accumulated cost ➔

cost

| Problem
definition | Feasibility
study | Analysis | System
design | Detailed
design | Implemen-
tation | Mainten-
ance |

must have an idea of what it will cost. Some sense of the likely cost/benefit ratio is essential.

The cost of a system accelerates as we move through the development process; this is another argument for using a careful, structured approach. An error detected during analysis means that a month or two of a systems analyst's time has been wasted. What if the error is not detected until the implementation stage? More time will have elapsed, and many more people will be involved; the cost of the wasted effort will be much higher. Even worse is the danger that a bad system will be installed in spite of crucial errors, simply because "We've already spent all this money, and we can't quit now." The methodical approach of structured systems analysis and design increases the likelihood that significant errors will be detected early.

As exit criteria from the system design stage, the analyst is often asked to outline several alternative solutions to the problem including, as a minimum, the following:

1. A low cost solution that does the job and nothing more.

2. An intermediate cost solution that does the job well, and is convenient for the user. This system may include several features that the user did not specifically request, but that the analyst, based on experience and knowledge, knows will prove valuable.

3. A high cost, "Cadillac" system, with everything the user could possibly want.

Supporting each alternative should be a system flow diagram or other system description, and an estimate of costs and benefits.

The system design phase ends with a choice. Perhaps, management or the user will decide that the benefits to be gained from this system are not worth the cost, or programming may be unable to support the system. Thus the project ends. If the system is worth supporting, one alternative will be selected. The systems analyst's description of this alternative will be used as a high level model for developing the physical system.

Detailed Design

As we move into *detailed design*, management, the user, and programming have agreed on a general strategy for solving the problem. We know, for example, what programs will be needed by this system. We have not begun to write the programs, nor have we given serious consideration to how they might be written, but we do know that a program will be needed to perform certain functions. We also know, again in general terms, what hardware will be required. The basic question that must be answered during detailed design is: *How, specifically, should the system be implemented* (Fig. Q.7)?

Consider, for example, the programs. During detailed design, the systems analyst must develop, (ideally with the help of the programming department) a set of specifi-

173

cations for each program. These specifications should contain enough detail to support writing the actual code. If the system calls for new hardware, hardware specifications must be written in a form acceptable to the purchasing department. Generally, during detailed design, the systems analyst must define each component of the system to whatever level of detail is required for the implementation step.

Until very recently, writing a computer program was considered a highly personal task. The programmer was given a rather broad, functional level overview of the program, and turned loose. Some time later, the program was finished. Sometimes it performed the necessary functions. Occasionally, a creative programmer produced a true "gem," exceeding everyone's expectations. All too often, however, the finished product was late, over budget, barely acceptable, and impossible to maintain. No one was satisfied: not the programmers, not the users, and certainly not management. Structured programming was, in part, a reaction to such inconsistent programmer performance.

When a structured approach to systems analaysis and design is used, one of our objectives is to develop program specifications that make it easy to write structured code. The HIPO technique (see Module H) is a popular tool for developing such specifications; Warnier/Orr diagrams (Module K) are an alternative.

The specifications developed during detailed design are analogous to the engineer's blueprints. Given these detailed specifications, it is possible to generate highly accurate cost estimates and implementation schedules, two factors extremely important to management. The programmers (more generally, those who will implement the system) will use the specifications to guide their actions. Finally, the user should be able to see an image of the finished system in the specifications.

Fig. Q.7: *Detailed design.*

Step	Key Question	Exit Criteria

Detailed design	How, specifically, should the system be implemented?	Implementation specifications
		  HIPO
		  pseudo code
		  Warnier/Orr diagrams
		Hardware specifications
		Cost estimates
		Preliminary test plan
		Implementation schedule

Implementation

During the *implementation* stage, the system is physically created (Fig. Q.8). Necessary programs are coded, debugged, and documented. New hardware is selected, ordered, and installed. What does the analyst do during implementation? Operating procedures must be developed. Security and auditing procedures will probably be required. The test plan must be established. It is easy to overlook the procedures and the test plan, but without these elements, there is no system. The implementation stage normally ends with a formal system test involving all components and procedures.

Maintenance

Following implementation, the system enters a *maintenance* stage. The objective of maintenance is to keep the system functioning at an acceptable level. Occasionally, program bugs will slip through the system test undetected; correcting such errors is a maintenance function. More often, the parameters and algorithms used to develop the original programs will change, meaning that the programs must be updated. Hardware maintenance is an obvious requirement. Even procedures change.

What does the systems analyst do during the maintenance stage? Typically, very little. In fact, it is likely that the analyst who designs a system will be working on another as the maintenance stage begins. The analyst does, however, have a significant impact on maintenance. Change may well be the only constant in the computer field; thus a well-designed system must anticipate and allow for change. Designing for change is the analyst's responsibility, and the structured approach to systems analysis and design tends to support this objective.

Fig. Q.8: *Implementation and maintenance.*

Step	Key Question	Exit Criteria

Implementation	Do it!	Programs
		  Code
		  Documentation
		Hardware
		Operating procedures
		Security procedures
		Auditing procedures
		Test plan
		Formal system test

Maintenance	Modify the system as necessary.	Continuing support

175

Fig. Q.9: *A summary of the structured systems analysis and design process.*

Step	Key Question	Exit Criteria
Problem definition	What is the problem?	Statement of scope and objectives
Feasibility study	Is there a feasible solution?	Rough cost/benefit analysis System scope and objectives
Analysis	What must be done to solve the problem?	Logical model of system Data flow diagram Data dictionary Algorithms
System design	How, in general, should the problem be solved?	Alternative solutions System flow diagrams Cost/benefit analysis
Detailed design	How, specifically, should the system be implemented?	Implementation specifications HIPO pseudo code Warnier/Orr diagrams Hardware specifications Cost estimates Preliminary test plan Implementation schedule
Implementation	Do it!	Programs Code Documentation Hardware Operating procedures Security procedures Auditing procedures Test plan Formal system test
Maintenance	Modify the system as necessary.	Continuing support

THE PROCESS

We have just covered the key steps in the structured systems analysis and design process (Fig. Q.9). Note the steady progression from the general to the specific. Note how we started with a purely logical view of the system, and gradually added details, layer by layer, until the physical system was implemented. This is an example of a top-down approach.

From our discussion, it might seem that the development of a system progresses smoothly, from step to step. Problem definition is followed by analysis; analysis by system design; in general, the end of one stage marks the beginning of the next. Unfortunately, it rarely happens that way. What happens, for example, if an error in problem definition is discovered during analysis? What if implementation difficulties force a change in design? A more realistic view of the process would map a less smooth path, with frequent returns to earlier steps. The important thing is that a sense of progression from step to step be maintained.

Monitoring the Process

Structured systems analysis and design defines a series of steps that must be followed in designing a system. Specific documentation standards exist for each step. How can we be sure that the analyst actually follows the process? It is essential that specific, measurable milestones or objectives be set for each step in the process. To be effective, such milestones must be enforceable. Many organizations use a formal inspection process, coupled with management reviews and the system test, to enforce the structured methodology. The inspections, management reviews, and the system test are summarized in Fig. Q.10. Formal inspections are described in Module A.

Fig. Q.10: *Key milestones in the systems analysis and design process.*

Step	Milestone
Problem definition	Management/user review
Feasibility study	Management review
Analysis	Inspection Management review
System design	Inspection Management review
Detailed design	Inspection Management review
Implementation	Inspection or walkthrough Formal test Management review

The Process and the Tools

Each step in the process calls for the completion of one or more specific documentation standards. It is easy to become bogged down in the details of this documentation. You may, for example, find yourself concentrating so heavily on completing the HIPO specifications for a single program, that you will lose sight of the overall process. Don't let that happen. Understand the process; that's the key. The individual documentation standards are details. You can learn how to use data flow diagrams, a data dictionary, a hierarchy chart, pseudo code, or any of the other tools described in this book; they are not difficult. Given enough practice, you will learn how to use the tools.

The process is different. It is almost a philosophy, a point of view. You can't really memorize it. Of course you can learn the names of the steps, but that's not the point. The idea is the smooth, methodical progression from the logical to the physical, from the top, down. This ability to sense the flow of the process, and to complete the documentation within the context of this process, is the essential skill of the systems analyst.

REFERENCES

1. Davis, William S. (1983). *Systems Analysis and Design: a Structured Approach*. Reading, Mass.: Addison-Wesley Publishing Company.

Sources

1. Atre, S. (1980). *Data Base: Structured Techniques for Design, Performance, and Management*. New York: John Wiley and Sons, Inc. **[E]**

2. Bohl, Marilyn (1978). *Tools for Structured Design*. Chicago: SRA. **[F,J]**

3. Brown, Rex V., Kahr, and Peterson (1974). *Decision Analysis for the Manager*. New York: Holt, Rinehart and Winston. **[O]**

4. Clifton, David S. and Fyffe (1977). *Project Feasibility Analysis: A Guide to Profitable New Ventures*. New York: John Wiley and Sons, Inc. **[C]**

5. Date, C. J. (1981). *An Introduction to Database Systems*, third edition. Reading, Mass.: Addison-Wesley Publishing Company. **[P]**

6. Davis, William S. (1983). *Operating Systems: a Systematic View*, second edition. Reading, Mass.: Addison-Wesley Publishing Company. **[M,P]**

7. Davis, William S. (1983). *Systems Analysis and Design: A Structured Approach*. Reading, Mass.: Addison-Wesley Publishing Company. **[Q]**

8. Fitzgerald, J., Fitzgerald and Stallings (1981). *Fundamentals of Systems Analysis*, second edition. New York: John Wiley and Sons. **[C,N]**

9. Foley, James D. and Van Dam (1982). *Fundamentals of Interactive Computer Graphics*. Reading, Mass.: Addison-Wesley Publishing Company. **[N]**

10. Freedman and Weinberg (1982). *Handbook of Walkthroughs, Inspections, and Technical Reviews*. Boston: Little, Brown and Company. **[A]**

11. Gane, Chris and Sarson (1979). *Structured Systems Analysis: Tools and Techniques*. Englewood Cliffs, New Jersey: Prentice-Hall, Inc. **[D,H,I]**

12. Gillett, Will D. and Pollack (1982). *An Introduction to Engineered Software*. New York: Holt, Rinehart and Winston. **[I]**

13. Gore, Marvin and Stubbe (1979). *Elements of Systems Analysis for Business Data Processing*, second edition. Dubuque, Iowa: Wm. C. Brown Company, Publishers. **[F,N]**

Source

14. Hartman, W., Matthes and Proeme (1968). *Management Information Systems Handbook.* New York: McGraw-Hill Book Company. [L]

15. Higgins, David A. (1979). *Program Design and Construction.* Englewood Cliffs, New Jersey: Prentice-Hall, Inc. [K]

16. IBM Corporation (1974). *HIPO—A Design Aid and Documentation Technique.* White Plains, New York: IBM Corporation. (Publication number GC20-1851). [H]

17. IBM Corporation (1977). *Inspections in Application Development—Introduction and Implementation Guidelines.* White Plains, New York: IBM Corporation. (Publication number GC20-2000). [A]

18. IBM Corporation (1974). *Introduction to IBM Direct-Access Storage Devices and Organization Methods.* White Plains, New York: IBM Corporation. (Publication number GC20-1649). [M]

19. Katzan, Harry Jr. (1976). *Systems Design and Documentation: An Introduction to the HIPO Method.* New York: Van Nostrand Reinhold. [H]

20. Kroenke, David (1977). *Database Processing.* Chicago: SRA. [E,P]

21. Lewis, T. G. and Smith (1976). *Applying Data Structures.* Boston: Houghton Mifflin Company. [M]

22. Lomax, J. D. (1977). *Data Dictionary Systems.* Rochelle Park, New Jersey: NCC Publications. Also distributed by Hayden Book Company. [E]

23. Martin, James (1977). *Computer Data-Base Organization,* second edition. Englewood Cliffs, New Jersey: Prentice-Hall, Inc. [P]

24. Orr, Kenneth T. (1981). *Structured Requirements Definition.* Topeka, Kansas: Ken Orr and Associates, Inc. [K]

25. Orr, Kenneth T. (1977). *Structured Systems Development.* New York: Yourdon, Inc. [K]

26. Parkin, Andrew (1980). *Systems Analysis.* Cambridge, Mass.: Winthrop Publishers, Inc. [N]

27. PERT Coordinating Group (1963). *PERT: Guide for Management Use.* Washington, D.C.: US Government Printing Office. (Publication number 0-69804520. [L]

28. Peters, Lawrence J. (1981). *Software Design: Methods and Techniques.* New York: Yourdon Press. [H,I]

29. Semprevivo, Philip C. (1982). *Systems Analysis: Definition, Process, and Design*, second edition. Chicago: SRA. **[F]**

30. Stewart, Charles J. and Cash (1978). *Interviewing Principles and Practices*, second edition. Dubuque, Iowa: W. C. Brown. **[B]**

31. Teichroew, D. (1964). *An Introduction to Management Science*. New York: John Wiley and Sons, Inc. **[G]**

32. Warnier, Jean-Dominique (1976). *The Logical Construction of Programs*. New York: Van Nostrand Reinhold. **[K]**

33. Warnier, Jean-Dominique (1978). *Program Modification*. London: Martinus Nijhoff. **[K]**

34. Weinberg, Gerald M. (1982). *Rethinking Systems Analysis and Design*. Boston: Little, Brown and Company. **[Q]**

35. Wiest, Jerome D. and Levy (1969). *A Management Guide to PERT/CPM*. Englewood Cliffs, New Jersey: Prentice-Hall, Inc. **[L]**

36. Yourdon, Edward and Constantine (1979). *Structured Design*. Englewood Cliffs, New Jersey: Prentice-Hall, Inc. **[D,H]**

Index